Potters

Oral History in the Staffordshire Ceramic Industry

Gordon Elliott
Gordon Elliott MA PhD

Acknowledgements

This book is the result of interviews with people who responded to my appeal in the Staffordshire Sentinel, made during the mid 1970s, for contributors to an oral record, a project that was, in part motivated by a wish to include commentaries in the then proposed displays to be housed in the extension to what was Hanley Museum, now the Potteries Museum.

As this intended use of the recordings did not materialise it would be most unfortunate if these life and work experiences were never to be made publicly available. The decision to publish some of the interviews has been made against this background. As well as providing an insight into an important area of local history, in particular ceramic manufacture, it is hoped that they will also serve as a modest tribute and memorial to those who were so generous in giving of their time and memories.

CHURNET VALLEY BOOKS
1 King Street, Leek, Staffordshire. ST13 5NW 01538 399033
thebookshopleek.co.uk
©Gordon Elliott and Churnet Valley Books 2004
ISBN 1 904546 19 6
Printed and bound by Bath Press

CONTENTS

A corner of Longton photographed by the author sometime during the early 1970s, a scene that looked less pleasing to the eye under smoke-filled skies.

INTRODUCTION

My long-standing interest in personal testimony was given added impetus during the mid 1970s as a result of private conversations with people who, by then long since retired, had at some time worked for differing periods in the ceramic industry of North Staffordshire. If they had one thing in common it was the richness of their individual experiences which fortunately they were usually able to recall with an impressive clarity. I was particularly conscious at this time of the sad fact that unless someone took the trouble to establish a permanent record of these memories valuable information would disappear with the holder's passing.

I was also concurrently carrying out research involving the use of documentary evidence compiled by Government Inspectors sent to the region in the mid-19th century to investigate conditions experienced by pottery workers, especially children. In the forefront of these investigations were Samuel Scriven and Robert Baker. Scriven had undertaken his survey in 1840s while Baker carried out a similar exercise in the early 1860s. What their investigations revealed was an industry in need of radical improvement, especially with regard to its attitude concerning the employment of children. Both Scriven and Baker interviewed child workers of both sexes who at the age of, for example, seven years were required to undertake heavy work that was invariably characterised by danger and by low or near non-existent pay.

It occurred to me at the time (the mid-1970s) that these children were, at least in chronological terms, of the same generation as the grandparents of the people I was holding conversations with. What I was told elicited the interesting and somewhat shocking evidence that little had been achieved in improving worker welfare during a period exceeding seventy years. Reading of the Scriven and Baker reports ran parallel with my then increasing interest in the writings of William Morris who, incidentally, had actually delivered a lecture in Burslem Town Hall in 1881 to which he gave the title 'The Art and Beauty of the Earth'. I suspect that Morris's intended audience was, ideally, those people for whom he had the greatest concern, essentially pottery workers possessing artistic aspirations who, as he saw it, were being exploited and dehumanised by monotonous routine. He was, of course, especially concerned about what he perceived to be the replacement of human labour by 'abominable machines'. In reality those who attended the lecture appear to have been the factory owners and others with a professional and perhaps cynical interest in his philosophy.

It was Morris's belief that most jobs in ceramic manufacture were exploitative and devoid of any creative satisfaction. One of my reasons for reading Scriven and Baker was to establish whether this was always and inevitably the case. Other sources suggest that this view of 19th century production was not entirely accurate. Indeed, Scriven's interviews with adult workers frequently reveal evidence indicating opportunities for self expression and even self improvement. Surprisingly, work that was routine and devoid of any obvious skills, often held for those involved a level of satisfaction that would not have been readily apparent to the casual observer. However, there were jobs in the industry that were inherently dangerous and without any opportunities for rewards material or otherwise, work that might have taken place in an environment of extreme heat, or conversely in conditions characterised by damp and cold; sliphouse procedures being an obvious example.

Attempts to establish parallels between 19th century manufacture and conditions and practices in the 20th century may at first sight appear invalid. The exercise perhaps takes on a greater relevance when it is recognised that many early 20th century practices had changed little in their fundamental principles over more than a hundred years.

The interviews that follow provide a mixture of information, some of it not entirely relevant to the subject of job satisfaction. As the work progressed my aims were widened, given the quality of the evidence being provided, so that what began as a project with a specific purpose in mind took on an extra dimension.

Oral history does however have its critics. They make the important point that anecdote cannot be easily corroborated and is therefore often of limited value. Past experience and an innate caution in these matters mean that I can readily sympathise with if not totally endorse this view. A good example of the pitfalls inherent in any alleged fact that cannot be independently verified is provided by the writings of a 19th century historian named Simeon Shaw. He states in the preface to his book, *History of the Staffordshire Potteries,* 1829: 'This volume originated in the reminiscences of many aged persons, who witnessed the time and manner in which the art of pottery had attained much of its importance.'

It is, however, unfortunate for Shaw's credibility and hence reputation as an historian, that many of his stories are little better than rumours. In his defence it must be said that he lived at a time when public libraries, as we know them today, didn't exist. Even if there had been a library in Shaw's time it would have contained very few books relevant to his subject, simply because they had not in the 1820s been written. A present day historian has access to avenues for investigation that would have been inconceivable even fifty years ago. The computer is perhaps the most obvious example of a highly sophisticated technology with immense potential for anyone engaged in research. In Shaw's case, because he lacked reliable documentary evidence, handed-down stories still in circulation were his only source.

A much more recent comment on this aspect of oral testimony is provided by Stephen Caunce in *Oral History and the Local Historian*, 1994. He writes, 'What I know I can vouch for, what someone else tells me, I can pass on with a comment on their reliability, but what I hear from someone who heard it from someone else is really just a rumour.' A further point that the collector of oral testimony should be aware of is that a contributor may have a wish to please, in other words tempted to give the interviewer details that they believe are expected or required. The only insurance against placing unwarranted reliance on such contributions is a strong grounding in the history and traditions of the subject under investigation. I believe I was on the whole fortunate in receiving quality evidence from people who were largely dispassionate and objective.

A further point that must be considered concerning the quality of the evidence being provided is in instances where the contributor appears to be so authoritative that whatever they say is beyond question. The words of an oral historian on this subject are again appropriate:

'Special care has to be taken where we are dealing with people who are used to managing interviews, for it encourages us to be uncritical, and even a desire to avoid causing offence can make bad history. If there is something which cannot be said, and there very rarely is, we must not bend the truth so as to be able to use a more acceptable version.'

I encountered only one instance during the course of my research where the person being interviewed provided information that challenged accepted opinion. This came from my conversation with a retired art education administrator named Reginald Tomlinson. At an early stage of Mr Tomlinson's career he worked for the art potter, Bernard Moore. In my interview with him he claimed that the credit for the rediscovery of a glaze effect known as flambe had been wrongly attributed to Moore. According to Mr Tomlinson's source, the man lodging the counter claim, namely a pottery painter named Wilkes, it was he who had made the discovery. Given Tomlinson's standing and eminence in the art world this information warranted serious consideration. It is worth mentioning that the manner of this contributor's presentation gave it a certain authority. An important point often mentioned by collectors of oral testimony is the significance of listening to a contributor (tape recording) as distinct from a transcript of their account. Even Samuel Scriven included interviews where he has written down statements of certain workers as they were delivered to him in local dialect, the broadness of which would have almost certainly rendered what was said incomprehensible to all but someone local to the area. In Mr Tomlinson's case the combination of his delivery, former occupation and later eminence as a portrait painter would appear to confer on his testimony a high level of reliability. However, in the introduction to my conversation with him I will explain why the Wilkes/flambe claim is open to doubt.

From the standpoint of representation and balance it is unfortunate that fewer women responded to my appeal for contributors than men. I suspect that what can only be interpreted as reticence might have been due to the unfortunate and unwarranted belief, on the part of many amongst the city's female population, that women's work was not either important or interesting enough to be worth recording for posterity, a situation that inevitably bestows a particular value on the oral testimony of those women who took part in the exercise. Mrs Alice Morris, for instance, recounts the poverty of her childhood and the contrasting satisfaction that resulted from employment as a lathe treader and scolloper in the town of Longton during the early years of the last century. An important aspect of this particular interview is the evidence it provides regarding the late application of steam power to a procedure that one might otherwise consider to have been an early beneficiary in the application of mechanical methods. A thrower that I interviewed, namely Mr George Myatt, revealed a parallel situation in connection with the practice of throwing.

Almost all those who took part in the project had at some time worked in the ceramic industry of Stoke on Trent. The single exception was the owner of a pawnshop in the city called Tildsley's, located in Marsh Street, Hanley. I felt the inclusion of a representative of this trade was very appropriate given the fact that many of those interviewed by

A smoky scene over Longton, photographed at the end of the 19th century by W.J. Blake.

Marl hole and pot banks at the beginning of the 20th century.

Government Inspectors in the 19th century and, indeed, most of the people who contributed to my research had, at times, reason to draw on the pawnbroker's services.

For Scriven and Baker in the 19th century their work had the added value that they actually visited their subject's place of employment. This is not always the case with present day oral history. A collector today does however have the tremendous advantage of easy access to modern recording methods. The popularity of television programmes, which include interviews with people who have played an important role in or witnessed a particular event in history, have generated a greater audience awareness of the value of oral testimony. I regret that when carrying out interviews in the 1970s video-recording equipment was not available in an affordable form, and cine cameras capable of producing results of good quality were beyond the means of all but those with an abundance of funds. Had photographic equipment been available in a suitably portable form to Scriven and, later, Baker, one can only imagine the graphic potential of their observations. Where possible I have included illustrations of places etc. that would bear reasonable comparison with the conditions experienced by my contributors.

I have to admit to being somewhat suspicious of an artist's impression. In assessing evidence of this kind it is important that one is aware of its intended purpose. A good example of the extent to which a sketch or painting may convey an over roseate impression is provided by a guide published by the Wedgwood firm in 1920, under the title of *Artes Etruriae Renascuntur*. Illustrated with drawings by James Hodgkiss, a designer at Wedgwood, it includes scenes based upon quaint corners of the factory. The guide in this instance provided Wedgwood enthusiasts with an impression of workshops characterised by an atmosphere of acceptable rustic decay. In reality what had been a classic example of industrial architecture and associated workers' cottages in 1769 was, by the late 1920s, sufficiently decayed and outdated to warrant the company's removal to a new site and the construction of accommodation more in keeping with 20th century requirements.

An interesting subject mentioned by most of my contributors was the usually good relationship between employers and workers. Mrs Morris went as far as to say that a good boss could be better than one's own father in circumstances of parental indifference or, in some instances, physical abuse. Historians have adopted the word paternalism to identify this kind of employer/employee relationship. That this degree of paternalism was not the norm for British industry at this time (the early 1900s) is reinforced by the following statement attributed to a Captain A. Sydenham of the Ministry of Labour writing in 1920, 'Employers in the pottery industry are still in direct personal contact with their workers to an extent that was unknown in many other industries.' This is a tradition that may be traced back to the early decades of the 19th century.

Some manufacturers extended their benevolence to the wider community. For example, the Ridgways, who owned pottery premises in Shelton, were instrumental in the construction of Hanley's Bethesda Chapel and schoolroom. Female members of the same family also taught at the chapel's Sunday School. Some employers went to great lengths to defend their welfarism. A descendant of the mid-19th century Ridgways opposed the National Insurance Bill in 1911 on the grounds that his own sick club scheme was better. In the early 20th century some of the larger employers funded 'Rest and Health' recreation clubs and 'Welfare Institutes'.

Other examples of paternalism in the industry include the Aynsley family's backing of Longton Cottage Hospital. Thomas Taylor gave an annual treat for the two hundred poorest children in Hanley, a gesture recorded in Pottery Gazette for the 1st February 1906. Some years later in 1918 the Misses Audrey and Phoebe Wedgwood called a meeting to discuss workers' housing. The year before, local manufacturers had raised funds to provide ambulances for the War effort. Major Frank Wedgwood, although then beyond the age for serving officers, was called upon during the 1914-18 War to act as a recruiting officer.

In my own youth I remember coming into contact, via National Service, with members of the Adams and Wedgwood families who were officers in the North Staffordshire Regiment. This link between the district's potting dynasties and military service was for some not always welcomed. George Myatt, mentioned earlier, left his job with Wedgwood of Etruria because having carried out military service himself, he resented what he perceived to be a military-like regime practised at the factory. He was also uneasy about what he termed the 'true blue Wedgwood' attitude associated with loyalty to the company's values.

There were other aspects of paternalism that were not always welcomed by the industry's employees. Some have argued that it weakened the power of the Pottery Workers' Union and gave rise to privately-negotiated wage agreements. It has been said that a position conferred by birth alone does not always lead to the most efficient direction and leadership. Certain interviewees believed that they had been personally disadvantaged because a less than able son had taken over some important aspect of the family business. Many family-owned firms have until recent times suffered from a lack of financial investment.

This handicap became especially apparent following the Second World War period with the industry's changeover from solid fuel firing to the firing of kilns with gas and electricity. The traditional bottle oven was found to be uneconomical and generally at odds with other areas of technical improvement. For instance, the firing cycle was inconveniently long. From the initial filling of the oven to the removal of finished wares could take up to a week. Developments on the Continent were being introduced before the end of the 19th century that involved the construction of a brick tunnel through which the wares on trucks would pass during firing. Perhaps the most obvious benefit arising from this invention was that firing could continue without shutting down the kiln at the end of each firing cycle. It was also much cleaner than the bottle oven in terms relating to conditions on the factory, and, perhaps, more importantly was what today would be classified as environmentally friendly.

At first the so-called 'Dressler oven', named after its inventor Conrad Dressler, was an option limited to the more prosperous manufacturers. The infamous smogs that reached a peak in the early 1950s were instrumental in the national government-inspired campaign to abolish, or at least control, the worst offending elements in the industries of the day. What had at first been presented as a desirable option became for ceramic manufacture compulsory. Unfortunately, for many of the smaller, under-financed, family owned businesses, the cost of installing a tunnel kiln was out of the question, with the result that many firms simply went out of business. Although known to have been handicapped by additional problems, one being the proposed construction of a bus station on its site, there can be little doubt that a firm mentioned in an interview to follow was indirectly a victim of the Act. I am referring to the small Longton factory of John Lockett, a remarkable example in the 1950s of a 19th century time capsule with its workshops converted from a row of cottages and a pub to its range of products which included pots for meat and tooth paste and jars for the storage of leeches. The decision made by Wedgwood to abandon its Etruria Works for pastures new (literally) on what was previously farmland belonging to the Barlaston estate, was in part based upon the need to construct a factory compatible with the needs of modern firing methods.

Photographic evidence produced in the early 1900s shows the Potteries towns to have been an area almost permanently covered by a thick veil of smoke, hardly an environment conducive to healthy living. The Duchess of Sutherland, in her summary of the state of the Six Towns in 1900, wrote, 'The Potteries is thus, and inevitably, mainly a place of muddy, squalid streets, insignificant public buildings, smoky atmosphere, potworks and rows of small houses. Nine tenths of its population are of the working class, and its well to do live mostly in their little colonies outside. Possibly the greatest advantage incidental to living in the Potteries is the hope of being able to make enough money to live out of it.'

In the Duchess's case she lived in the salubrious and leafy surroundings of the Trentham estate. At the time of her writing the Sutherlands were amongst the most wealthy of the nation's ruling aristocracy. While few could have matched the magnificence of the Duchess's living arrangements many of the district's more affluent manufacturers headed at the end of the working day for their homes south of the Potteries towns at locations in the environs of Newcastle and Trentham. Others went home to the agricultural areas of Endon, Longsdon and Rudyard.

As a special treat for their workers some of the factory owners of the early 1900s organised annual summer garden fetes complete with children's entertainers such as Punch and Judy, and perhaps a merry go round. Such events might have been for some a source of envy and unrest. This however appears generally not to have been the case, as revealed during the course of carrying out my interviews. There were some factory owners for whom the workplace became less of a direct responsibilty perhaps to be visited on no more than two or three occasions in the course of a month. By the 1920s more firms were employing what was termed 'jacket men'. These were managers and foremen elevated in status by being placed on the staff. It was not uncommon for someone promoted in this way to relinquish their union membership. In the present context the importance of their role lay in them being able to take over the administrative responsibilities that were previously the preserve of the factory owners.

An important area of my investigations concerned the prevalence of industrial illnesses resulting from workers' exposure to ceramic materials that were found to be dangerous, in particular calcined flint and lead oxide. In their mid-19th century reports both Scriven and Baker came across numerous instances of workers adversely affected by these materials. For example, during Scriven's visit to the manufactory of Minton and Boyle he interviewed a forty-one years old scourer named Annie Williams. She told Scriven:

Happy pottery workers circa 1930s.

Canal and bottle kilns in Longport

'I have worked as a potter altogether 20 years. I have worked in this employ about 4 years. I am married, and have one girl who works on the same premises: I have two rooms in this department, and have 6 persons working with me. We never have children working with us. We receive our ware from the ovens in a dusty and rough state. Our business is to scour it with sand paper and stone. This occupation is very unhealthy, it stuffs a person up very much in the stomach, not many scourers live long, it takes some off sooner than others. None of us are ill now, except that we all feel overloaded upon the chest. Sometimes we cough very much, especially in the morning when we first begin. We are paid by the pieces and earn upon average 8 shillings or 9 shillings a week.'

Scriven reports: 'These rooms are spacious and have the means of ventilation. Particles of dust as in the sifting room adjoining the saggar room and oven are flying in all directions, the air is loaded with it.'

There are many other examples in his report of interviews with workers, including children, where exposure to silica led them to develop silicosis or as it was known potters' rot. Several people interviewed during my investigations made reference to having seen many suffering from the adverse effects that resulted from working with calcined flint or silica. For instance, in the period 1950 to 1959 almost 800 pottery workers died with silicosis or pneumoconiosis given as the primary cause of death, with 2,421 new cases being recorded during the same period. Even in the present day ceramic industry, despite the provision of dust extraction systems, silicosis continues to be an occupational hazard. Unlike other materials, lead for example, there is no satisfactory substitute for calcined flint. Those interviewees who mentioned silicosis attributed the problem to a variety of causes, ranging from the bad habits of certain workers to the lack of adequate ventilation, and the fettling and turning of wares that had been left to dry to a white state.

A subject less often mentioned was lead poisoning perhaps for the obvious reason that I did not interview anyone who had been directly involved with the glazing stage of manufacture. However, given that all my contributors, despite having worked in the industry around the time of or before the First World War, felt that it was not a major issue came as something of a surprise. Lead poisoning had been such a serious problem in the earthenware sector of manufacture that the Government drew up a set of rules under Section 79 of the Factory and Workshop Act, 1901. The Act ran parallel with experiments to discover an alternative to lead for the production of glazes and enamels. In due course glaze chemists were able to formulate compositions for which they adopted the term low solubility. The all important characteristic of these new glazes was that they were largely based upon borosilicate frits that were free from any seriously toxic properties. They were safe to use from the pottery workers' standpoint and posed no threat to the consumer.

Scriven's report contains numerous descriptions of people who were seriously affected by lead poisoning. Lead could cause blindness, a condition known as drooped wrist and, in pregnant women workers, the danger of abortion. The abortive properties of lead were so widely recognised that it was made into a pill form and supplied, illegally, to those who wished to terminate a pregnancy. One interviewee who had witnessed in others at least their exposure to glazes containing lead recalls her employer's provision of a daily quota of milk in the belief that it possessed palliative properties.

The application of regulations conducive to worker welfare, especially with regard to health problems, was made more difficult by the tradition of employing sub contract labour. In practice this meant that, for example, a thrower might employ his wife or daughter to turn the wheel, someone else as a 'taker off' to remove wares to the greenhouse, and maybe his son, or even another daughter to wedge the clay. Regulations introduced shortly before 1900 saw the replacement of small boys for wedging duties by young women. He, the thrower, was accordingly responsible for paying out members of his work team. Interviewee George Myatt describes this system of employment in connection with his work for John Lockett's factory.

One practice that was the cause of ongoing disputes from the time of its introduction in the late 18th century to its eventual abolition in 1919 was a method of wage calculation based upon 'good from oven', in other words any items that were judged to be sufficiently defective, hence unsaleable, after firing were not paid for irrespective of the source of the problem. The carelessness or misjudgement of a single worker could, under this system, deprive several of his or her colleagues the rewards of their labour, despite them having performed their particular responsibilities to an acceptable standard. From 1919 good from oven was limited to the sanitary ware branches of the industry, a situation that lingered on until the practice was finally brought to an end in 1964.

Several people that I interviewed, some of whom are not included in the transcripts that follow, recall having to pay for certain items of equipment and materials necessary for the performance of their duties. Mouldmakers might have been expected to provide their own soft soap, paintresses their pencils, and in the case of George Myatt, the gas to illuminate his workshop.

A reason for arranging the interviews was an awareness during the 1970s that the industry was undergoing a radical transition. Many of the family-owned businesses that had existed in some cases since the 19th century were either closing down or being absorbed by larger concerns. This shrinkage of the industry was, in part, attributable to the previously mentioned abolition of bottle oven firing. Wedgwood, for example, took over Coalport in 1959, and in 1968 Johnson Brothers. Allied English Potteries was merged with Doulton and Co. in 1971. The tile manufacturing company H&R Johnson acquired the previously merged firms of Richard Tiles Ltd and Campbell Tiles Ltd in 1968. The practice of out sourcing, that has seen both Wedgwood and Doulton expand to production bases in South East Asia, was anticipated as early as the 1950s when Johnsons opened a factory in Australia in 1957, and in 1961 Twyfords expanded into South Africa. The latter company had previously established a production foothold in India. Overseas competition in the form of lower priced wares, that are perhaps of high quality, combined with a strong pound, will no doubt unfortunately shrink the Staffordshire ceramic industry further.

The possible fate of ceramic manufacture in this country is a situation mirrored in the other once important industries of steel manufacture, coal mining and textiles. However, while much has been lost, never to be revived, the towns that constitute the City of Stoke on Trent can be justly proud of a unique artistic heritage. With the possible exception of 18th and 19th century London's luxury trades of cabinet making, silver smithing, textiles and even ceramic production few regions of Britain can equal the city's rich tradition of skills and artistic achievement.

In carrying out the following interviews my aim was not to achieve a comprehensive record of workers' experiences representative of every branch of ceramic production. The project was undertaken in order to determine whether, despite the documented hardship of those involved, work in the ceramic industry could, for some, have in any sense been spiritually rewarding. With few notable exceptions pottery workers have virtually always been paid significantly below the national average. However, almost without exception my contributors recalled with an obvious nostalgia their memories of living and working in the Potteries. It was equally the case that whilst not necessarily having personally experienced hardship or even poverty they had witnessed these problems in others. In terms of my own agenda the exercise revealed the interesting fact that contrary to the views of 19th century critics of industry, and its associated practices, even the seemingly tedious routine was occasionally for those involved a rewarding experience.

A smoky view over the Potteries, circa 1910, from a negative by the
Longton-based photographer, W.J. Blake.

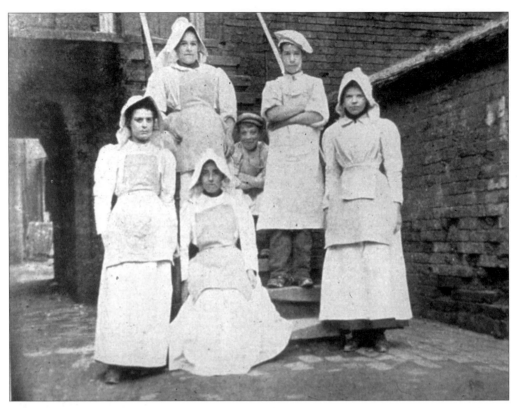

Ware dippers wearing protective clothing as a precaution against contamination from lead used in most ceramic glazes until its replacement by safer materials during the 1920s.

A view of a scene on Wedgwood's Etruria factory,
from a drawing by James Hodgkiss, early 20th century.

Wedgwood Factory frontage and the canal at Etruria, from a drawing by James Hodgkiss, who was employed as a designer at Wedgwood during the early decades of the last century.

Below:
Perhaps a somewhat more realistic representation of a typical factory at the end of the 19th century. Note the external staircases which were frequently coated with wet clay, an ever present hazard for factory workers.

Reginald Haggar mentions the crowded displays he found at Hanley Museum upon his arrival
in the Potteries in 1929. When I joined the museum in the early 1950s the main ceramic
displays were virtually identical to the arrangement shown here.

Reginald Haggar
Painter, Author and Lecturer.

Interviewed at Hanford, Stoke on Trent, 1976.

I first met Reginald Haggar in the 1950s when as a very junior member of the Hanley Museum staff I was called upon to assist him in connection with the selection of pots, either for some publication that he was then working on, or for the purpose of illustrating a lecture. He was also at this time a leading figure in the Society of Staffordshire Artists, and a regular contributor to its annual exhibition of members' work then displayed in the old Russell Gallery in Pall Mall, Hanley.

Reginald Haggar was born on Christmas Day in 1905 at Ipswich in Suffolk. His natural abilities as a painter led him to attend the town's school of art followed by his acceptance by the Royal College of Art to study 'pictorial design'. Then as now making a living through the sale of one's artistic work was dependent on a combination of fortuitous circumstances. In the period following the First World War the market for paintings, especially those done in watercolour, was either sporadic or limited to the work of those who had already established a reputation. At this point, even in the town of his birth, Haggar's reputation was in its early stages. It no doubt became apparent that if he wished to take his career further his undoubted artistic talents would have to be steered in the direction of industrial design.

This aspect of his career began in 1929 when he was offered the post of Assistant Designer at the Stoke-based firm of Minton. A change of job title confirms at least his credentials for the job for within six months of being appointed he was promoted to become Minton's Art Director. However, subsequent events suggest the role of ceramic designer was not entirely compatible with Haggar's temperament and ambitions for in 1935 he recalls 'I left in the middle of the week without notice. I knew that if I did not go myself they would have given me the sack', a decision that prompted him to enter the field of art and design education. He was appointed Head of Stoke School of Art, a position which he held until 1941, before moving to a similar position as art school head in the nearby town of Burslem. In 1945 he in turn resigned his post at Burslem School of Art to become a full time artist, writer and lecturer.

As a frequent visitor to the City Museum and Art Gallery, Hanley, both privately and in his role as President of the Northern Ceramic Society, I found Reginald Haggar to be a unique source of information on many aspects of British ceramic history, especially that relating to what is recognised as the beginnings of the industrial period (1770-) to the industry of his own lifetime. Interviewing Mr Haggar was made easy by the fact that what follows had, on occasions, been presented as a lecture, albeit unscripted, for the numerous adult education groups to which he was a frequent contributor.

Reginald Haggar's reputation as a ceramic historian is well-known via a combination of published work, the lecture programmes he provided for the Adult Education Department of Keele University and his Presidency of the Northern Ceramic Society.. In addition to numerous magazine articles and reviews, his published works include:

English Pottery Figures 1660-1860

English Country Pottery

The Masons of Lane Delph

A Century of Art Education in the Potteries

Staffordshire Chimney Ornaments

The Concise Encyclopedia of Continental Pottery and Porcelain

The Concise Encyclopedia of English Pottery and Porcelain with Wolf Mankowitz

Mason Porcelain and Ironstone 1796-1853 with Elizabeth Adams

Each autumn a memorial lecture in his name is staged at the Potteries Museum.

Reginald Haggar's death occurred on 4 December 1988 at Wetley Abbey Nursing Home near Leek in Staffordshire. There is a sense of morbid appropriateness here in that the subject of one of Reginald Haggar's books was the potter George Miles Mason, who lived there from circa 1831. Haggar's reference to its neo-gothic appearance is in keeping with his self-proclaimed love of 'old crumbling buildings' and a liking for 'desolation and dereliction'.

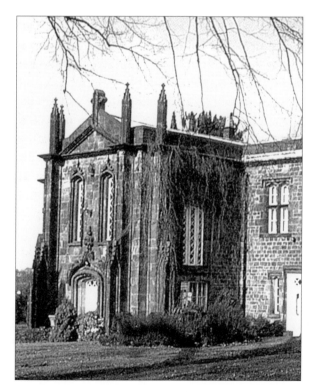

Someone once described Reginald Haggar to me as possessing something of the Gothic, and I know myself that he had a liking for the bleakness of churchyards. He loved Wetley Abbey (left), and it is described in the book he co-authored with Elizabeth Adams, *Mason Porcelain & Ironstone 1796-1833* (Faber 1977):

"By 1829, the increasing success of the Mason firm enabled George Miles (Mason) to retire from business and he was able to enjoy the leisured life of a wealthy man at Wetley Abbey, the neo-gothic mansion he purchased from William Adams in 1831."

In the 1980s Wetley Abbey became a nursing home, and it was by strange coincidence that in his last years Haggar became a resident there and died in 1988 in the house he loved.

Reginald Haggar

When I came here in August of 1929 it was pouring with rain. I got a very dim impression of the place coming in from London on the Derby line. The place was extremely dirty and dark. I was met at Stoke Station by a fellow student, a local artist named Leonard Brammer[1], a native of the Potteries. He asked me where I was going to live and I said I'm not going to live in this ruddy hole. I went out on the first train to Stone.

It's only in the course of time that I've gradually moved in towards the Potteries and come to live in the Potteries itself. At that time Stoke was a very grim place. Indeed, of the six towns I suppose the worst. It's a town without very much character; it never had much more than its factories and its railway stations and therefore it didn't create an impression with me of anything that was attractive. One felt there was only a life that was associated either with the church or chapel, which of course was very evident, but more particularly with the major factories of which there were only two important ones that impinged on the eye. They were the big factory of Spode, which occupied an enormous area, and Minton's.

At that time I came to Minton to be a designer, in the first instance, but in fact I became Art Director within six months. Minton then had three different factories on the banks of the canal, the earthenware factory and the china bank, and the old stone bank where they made tiles and majolica vases and ornamental wares. It was here that a good deal of experimental work on electric kilns took place with Moore Campbell, and led to the first electric tunnel oven coming in to the Potteries, which had been installed two years before I came, at Wedgwood's.[2]

At that time when I came to Minton it was a very dreary old factory. I had a little room in the art director's studio. It was exactly like it was in the time of Leon Arnoux, whose portrait hung on the wall.[3] He was a bearded old man. The water jars that were used were the same jars that were on the table in the portrait of Arnoux. The walls were black, not with paint but with dirt. It had not been painted since Arnoux's time. All the furnishings were exactly as they were in the 19th century, the great bench all round the big room with its two windows facing the canal and three on the main road. Underneath those benches were piles and piles of drawings which I loved to go through because they were the drawings of Alfred Stevens, Reuter and all the great artists that would have been at Minton's during the 19th century. On the walls were pictures by Mucha. He was one of the avante garde artists of the period and I am sure that they were, as it were, Solon's pin-ups, and influenced him in his later work; and like Mucha he went to America.[4]

The centre table was always covered with pots, mostly pots that were put on one side because they mustn't go into the warehouse and be thrown away. They could always be salvaged for heavy elaborately gilt patterns of a sort which cover up a multitude of sins. The sorting you know for an expensive plate is not the kind of sorting that you need for a plain white plate which is more difficult to make. So this was a place where a good deal of salvage operations took place.

Minton at that time was not a factory where any progress had been revealed in the actual planning or development of the factory. It was a ramshackle old place and the toilets down on our end of the factory, by the art director's, were so foul that we always hoped that when American buyers came they would be taken, as it were, suddenly so that something would be done about them. It was as bad as that, and throughout the whole of the old factory there was a feeling that these belonged essentially, you know, to Victorian times. The old traditions were upheld and maintained without alteration into the period when I came to the factory.

Of course at that time the factory was undergoing a lot of changes. Its trade, which was all in America, the china trade, was affected most powerfully by the Wall Street collapse in 1929-30. In the aftermath Minton's really were losing money very heavily. They were quite obviously finding it difficult to produce enough to fill the kilns which they had at that time and so no progress could be made.

But the most interesting part of the setup, as I see it now in memory, was the recollection of the view down from the art director's room which looked down on the canal and the Gordon Mill, which was along that road that passes by Minton at the present time. The canal path went underneath it. I did make a drawing at that time, I don't know where it has got to nowadays, but it would be rather a document of what Stoke was like at that time. The Stone Bank was in a state of dereliction, very little was done on the Stone Bank and indeed most of the factory was given over to Mr Arthur J. Campbell who was certainly I think a man of some genius.[5] He was, I believe, responsible with Major Moore for the Moore Campbell electric kiln. He was working on a new principle of electric kiln at that time in which the wares would go on runners, which worked perfectly, and then failed as experiments often do. I think it was a matter of great distress to Arthur Campbell who subsequently left. He was managing director before he went to Rhodesia where he died.

There were some very interesting old tiles and pattern books to be found amongst the rubbish on the Old Stone Bank. The china factory extended the full length of London Road, and was known as quarter-mile Minton. It went on and on and the Campbell Tile Company butted on to it, and was much the same in its general appearance. It did seem quite endless on that side, the dreariest facade in the whole of the Potteries, three storeys broken by the central bay which was four storeys. It may have had a coat of paint put on it during its lifetime but if it did I can't remember. It was rather like the interior, grim and dark. On the other side of the road was the earthenware bank which faced the road. There were the old showrooms, and the office block, again very Victorian. Behind that was the old factory, the old earthenware factory, which was a very ramshackle sort of place in all directions. Very little repair work had been done to this factory, although they had installed concrete floors and a tunnel kiln for firing earthenware. I do remember seeing a girl come through the ceiling from one floor into the room below. She wasn't hurt one was glad to say but it showed how little had been done to repair or maintain the place. Indeed, as long as the buildings stood it was alright. Minton's earthenware wasn't very exciting but nevertheless they had a considerable trade in the European market at that particular time.

My first impression of the Potteries, from outside the factory, was that the people of the Potteries looked so clemmed and starved if you can use the two words that cover hunger and cold, they looked pinched, wan and ill. I remember that every lunchtime I went to

Hanley Museum. It was my way of spending the lunchtime. I used to go up and at the bus station one would see people, some of which were going up to the orthopaedic at Hartshill with children strapped on boards in days when none of the amenities or remedies for those who were handicapped and sick were available. The area had that dark, sombre look which seemed to me almost as though I was witnessing something in a dream because it was totally different from the world that we know, of course, of the Potteries today. I came up to the museum, as I said, and loved the collections that were on show. If I might put this in I think that the collections were then displayed far better that they are today, or shall I say far better than they were before the new museum was started, because they had nearly everything in the museum, and you could see them. Now, when they open cases and put things on display they generally put one piece in a case, and a label on it if they know what it is. There was a sort of feeling of fullness and richness in the museum which was like the life of the people.[6] You could go and see what they made and there wasn't a great deal of discrimination as to the quality of the things that were put on display.

The people of the Potteries were immensely proud. They have some reason to be proud. Coming to the district I was very conscious of their pride in their craftsmanship, and you know "nobody could do it like I could do it or my father could do it. He was better than I was". It was that kind of approach and, indeed, many of those who were working as artist craftsmen were intensely skilled people. They were immensely proud of it, and again this of course is something that is always told you by strangers that they are extremely hospitable, and they are, and they are not afraid to tell you that they are very hospitable. This is again a characteristic of people who live within that small world of the Potteries which I experienced when I came. I received a lot of friendship and a lot of helpfulness from the people at that time.

I think there was a certain class consciousness amongst the workers; it was shown in a curious way. I don't mean there was snobbery but I remember vividly that the artists and gilders always seemed to be a little apart from those who were the white workers, working in the clay even if they were fine craftsmen. The sort of symbol of it I can remember was one particular artist at Minton, I won't name him but he always had pin-striped trousers and a rather smart black jacket, and a turned-down collar with a little black bow tie. He looked really something of course but there was nothing underneath it, it was only a facade.

The first taste of clean air in the Potteries really starts at the period of the Wall Street collapse. So many of the great factories, particularly in Stoke, were deeply affected because their trade was in the American market, largely, or almost exclusively in the case of Minton's for their china.

Their ovens were closing down, not operating in the same way as they did before. The tendency was for the atmosphere to become rather cleaner than it had been before, and I feel sure that this is the point when the modern development of the pottery industry starts because at that time it reached rock bottom, as far as trade was concerned. It also was a period when innovation and change in design began and was forced upon the industry, although perhaps not in the direction of anything particularly modern. There was a greater concentration upon simplified shapes and designs to meet a requirement of a public which could not afford the expensive goods that had been produced before. I don't think we have realised the full extent of that slump. It's something that has never been experienced in the industry since, and certainly could not be matched at any period before the battle of Waterloo. Then for five years the whole of the industry suffered much the same kind of way because the whole of the European and world markets were closed to British pottery manufacturers. Those that were open, like Russia, didn't pay for the goods that they received. That was also disastrous in its own way.

The slump meant a great decline in the number of pottery workers because those who had been gilders and painters at the great factories (most of them had an army of such people on their staff) began to walk the streets. In fact in the end the great gilding workshop of Minton's was a skeleton, a bare, meagre skeleton of what it was at the very beginning. Those that remained were not the most skilled workers but they were the ones who could do the simplest tasks in the most select and easy manner.

There was a trimming of the industry and after that men went into other trades and, indeed, perhaps one of the great changes brought about by it was an increased local awareness in the Potteries of the necessity to get other industries besides Michelin into the area.[7] It was believed that the work could be shared out, and those who were unemployed could find jobs, perhaps even better paid jobs than in the pottery industry itself. I'm sure it was beneficial to the industry as a whole because it tended to set competitive standards of welfare on factories, and the amenities of factories, and of course for salaries and wages. So there was a blessing as well as a curse in the great slump.

Those who walked the streets, amongst the more skilled craftsmen, wanted to be independent as far as they could of the dole. It was not uncommon to find artists hawking their designs from factory to factory asking for what we were willing to give them, a half crown or even a shilling. "Take some please if you possibly can. I know they may be no good to you at the moment but if you could only take some it would help us." One did perhaps buy half a dozen designs and stick 'em in the waste paper basket. At best it helped the poor individual who had nothing to look forward to.

One of the things most striking about the industry was that much of the ware produced was in a stereotyped form of decoration. There was nothing modern, nothing fresh being made in the industry. You see the 1930s was the period of what they call Art Deco. The rising figures were those of Susie Cooper and Clarice Cliff who made reputations in their particular field for their, I would say in the case of Clarice Cliff at any rate, crude colourings.[8] The fine china manufacturers were not really receptive to anything of that kind and, indeed, the refinement of their products didn't lend itself very easily to it. One feels that all the major factories at that particular time tended to be looking backwards. They were producing variations of standard designs rather than venturing into new fields. But, of course, if you look at what is being produced today (1976) in the pottery industry they expect of Mason, Mason's designs, they expect of Wedgwood, Wedgwood designs. They say you can go to the Continent to get modern designs. There has been that constant battle I think through almost every age in the modern period to innovate, on the one hand, by those younger members who come into the industry, and to conserve, hold back as it were, by those in power in the manufacturing world.

There had been an advance in design during this period. I noticed it very markedly that there was a better feeling for shapes than there was before, and designs tended to be more refined than they were before, although perhaps a great many of those that were adopted in the industry, by some of the fine china groups, tended to be what I would call anaemic good design, in other words a kind of refined taste that had no dynamic power. This, I think, had been lacking from the time of the Industrial Revolution. Indeed, if you go back to the period, of what I will call classical kinds of design you have to go back to before 1820.

G.W.E. Were the people that you recruited to do the gilding and painting given any prior art training in schools of art, or did they come straight into the industry from ordinary schools?

R.H. A lot of them came out of the apprentices at the factory. Some, of course, came from the art schools but obviously they couldn't supply all the requirements of an industry at that time. The art schools were very effective in producing, shall we say, the young apprentice modeller. On the whole I think a great many of them came into the industry because their father had been in the industry before them. This gives rise to what I call the dynasties, the generations of a family that go on and on producing and working in the same kind of family tradition. This can lead to an immense pride but it also led to a kind of repetition because some did what their father did, sometimes better but generally speaking not quite as good.

There were some very striking personalities in the pottery industry when I came. I remember very vividly old Alfred Meigh who often called at the works. He and Joe Hartley, the engineer, and old John Campbell, whom I think I've mentioned, were great friends. I can also remember not only the appearance of Alfred Meigh with his cape and his cap, his little carpet bag, his big boots and his knickerbockers. I remember that he had all the stories he liked to relate on his cuff so that he wouldn't forget them. He was, of course, at that time very interested in what he called semis, the back marks you find on pottery, which have been of great value to ceramic historians in helping to identify the products of different factories.[9]

G W.E. What was Alfred Meigh's occupation?

R.H. I'm not sure whether he had something to do with the supply industry that the family were concerned with at the time. He was probably too old at the time to be still working. I think he was pursuing as it were his hobbies. One thinks too of people like Moorcroft, William Moorcroft, who was a great personality, a very striking personality. He was very much the artist and very conscious of his quality as an artist. It was men of that kind that one can recollect amongst the working potters. I feel that some of the quality, the character which we associated with those men, who were very individualistic, has gone. That the new type of potter, the pottery engineer, is, shall we say, lacking in those individualistic qualities which I found so much the attraction of the Potteries. They seemed to reflect the buildings, and the buildings reflected them, they were part of a particular world.

I don't think, perhaps, that the generation coming into the industry today will feel about the Potteries quite the same as I did. I hated it but I found somehow that this hate of the Potteries soon resulted in a kind of love/hate relationship until finally love triumphed over the hate, and one found oneself involved completely as part of a community, a small world, and that world, I think, has broken down. After all is said and done the atmosphere of the Potteries is not all that much different from the atmosphere outside the area. It is different but not much different, and as you look at what is happening in the Potteries today it's very much like what is happening in many other towns and cities. At the very end of all the transformation that's taking place it will leave the area looking like any other old town anywhere in England. Instead of the little world that I particularly loved, which had its own individuality, a world which was comprised of the little towns and villages, each in rivalry one with the other which, of course, gave rise to its special characteristics. I can remember talking to a pottery artist in the district, and I said, "you know Stoke had a great reputation for the people who went to the School of Design."[10] "Hanley had a better reputation" was his immediate reply. It was that kind of rivalry which gave to the towns their special quality, their special flavour.

G.W.E. How long did it take you to come to terms with the apparent ugliness of Stoke?
R.H. I think that's very difficult to answer because it was such a gradual process, but certainly by the late thirties. You see I came in 1929. By the middle of the 1930s I was beginning to do some of the bottle ovens which somehow or another I got a reputation for depicting in more recent times. One of the very big panoramic views I did of the Potteries, which is now I think in the showroom of John Maddock of Burslem, does reflect my love of all the places, particularly in Burslem because it's done from the roof of Maddock's factory."[11]

The bottle ovens, most of which have gone, plus the church, that lovely church. I was so sorry to see it pulled down in Dalehall.[12] No , I was coming to terms with the area in the 1930s. The love had already developed for this particular world. It's an area of waste land. Waste lands that are very beautiful you know. I've never quite understood why people should resent the slag heaps unless, of course, perhaps you have experienced living in the shadow of them. From a visual point of view the slag heaps are magnificent, as magnificent as mountains, and so are the waste lands. One of the characteristics of the Potteries is the feeling of waste lands.'[13] In places we are taking up our churchyards, removing all the gravestones, we're tidying it all up and putting down nice lawns. It's not the Potteries. The Potteries is dereliction. The Gladstone Museum, for example, is a nice museum but a museum that no more reflects the pottery industry than any other museum. It's all too tidy, too respectable. I know that you might have an accident if you had a lot of rubbish about but that's what a potbank was like. You look at the old photographs and you see the outside staircases all covered with slush, slurry and muck. One wonders that nobody broke their neck. This is something that is rather controversial because it means that you've got to eliminate all your ideas of modern hygiene, and you've got to think in terms of what it was like in those days when men often had their meals at the bench, taking in the dust and clay and the lead with their food as they did.

In the 19th century they were warned against it by Dr Harley and others. Nevertheless, they went on in their ways because father had done it, and because they couldn't change. This is the way of the potter, reluctant to change. The employer was also very reluctant to change. The working potters resisted any change to their habits until change was forced upon them and, indeed, the real industrial revolution didn't take place in the 19th century, it took place at the very end of the Second World War. At that time there was so much needed that they had to reorganise the industry, and more rationalisation, more change, more modern methods, more techniques came in in the period just after the war and afterwards. This is when, as far as the pottery industry was concerned, the real industrial revolution took place.

G.W.E. At what point did you enter art education in the area?

R.H. It happened when I was Art Director of Minton's in the 1930s. Gordon Forsyth came to me one day and said Harry Tittensor, who was head of the School of Art, is leaving and would I take it on?[14] I said it depends on circumstances. We discussed it and I told him the terms on which I would come, and they were terms that suited me at that particular time. So I entered art education. I was very glad of it, financially of course. At that time Minton's were not fine payers, not in the 20th century.[15] I was also glad of it because it brought me into contact more directly with young designers and artists. I found teaching something which I have greatly loved ever since. Indeed, it's something I am going to miss as I leave the district.[16] I think it is beneficial to those who are involved in industry and in art generally because it means that they not only design but they have to think about the nature of design in order to explain it to other people. They are, therefore, probably more intelligent in their approach to the problems of designing. They begin to question the values which they hold and to challenge them, and to have them challenged. It's a good thing, I think, for the creative artist in any sphere. I've never regretted my experiences in the art schools. Mind you, it led to friction. You know, in the older days, if you was a Minton's artist you was a Minton man and they tended to regard you as theirs, and feel that if you did something else you were disloyal. A more absurd idea I've never heard, but at the same time it was very characteristic of the Potteries.

   To some extent, of course, there was a fear, a great fear, that those who had been concerned with the factory might leave them and pass their ideas on to other people. There was this feeling of the privateness of their own methods and techniques, skills and knowledge, and that they belonged exclusively to them. Nobody else could have it, in fact nobody else was able to match it. This, I feel, put a great fear into the hearts of many manufacturers, and it led to men being too restricted. It led to suspicions on the part of manufacturers of the art schools. "Why should we send our people to the art school where, in fact, they will be bettered and improved and we shall have them for about three months before they go off and work for somebody else, and give their ideas to new people?" It was that kind of spirit which was very rife at the time when I came into the industry here.

G.W.E. Is it possible to say whether the course of your work or style in painting would have been different had you not come to Stoke on Trent and gone to some other part of the country?

R.H. Well, that I think is impossible to answer because what on earth brought me to the Potteries in the first place? A job turned up and I took it and came here. I had no idea what the Potteries was like. I came from Suffolk, from country which was familiar with John

Constable and Thomas Gainsborough and the East Anglian school. I think possibly had I gone on from there I might have developed as a painter painting works in the tradition of Crome and John Sell Cotman who were, indeed, strong influences in the early days of my work. I might have been painting pastoral subjects, a different kind of world but I'm not sure about this because even when I was in my home town of Ipswich I loved the old, crumbling buildings and liked a sense of desolation and dereliction.

It may well be that change and decay are something that is inherent in my own nature, because, strange as it may seem I have several sketchbooks which are completely filled up with studies of gravestones. I like this rather strange world you know. I think it is the sense of decline and decay. It may even be the sense of decline and decay in the pottery industry which has been a major factor in focusing attention upon the evidence of man's past in the bottle kilns and the factories.

I think that is possibly the answer. Change is always taking place, but I suspect that what might be regarded as a decline, from the older type of industry, was taking place already before the Wall Street slump took place. That actually was the one point, historically, when evidence of change of which I've been talking was accelerated and increasingly took place.

Notes

1.   Leonard Griffith Brammer studied at Burslem School of Art 1921-26, was Master in Charge of Longton School of Art 1931-37, Art Master, Longton High School 1937-53. 1953 appointed Supervisor of Art in Schools, City of Stoke on Trent.

2.   Although Bernard Moore was experimenting with electrical firing as early as 1907 the industrial application of firing with electricity did not materialise until some twenty years later when Arthur J. Campbell and Bernard Moore junior introduced a tunnel kiln for firing enamel-decorated wares at Wedgwood's Etruria factory. Firing biscuit and glossed wares with electricity posed technical problems that were not resolved until the late 1930s.

3.   Leon Arnoux was Minton's Art Director from 1848 to 1892. He had originally been persuaded by Herbert Minton to leave the French Sevres factory with an offer of a generous salary and the position of Art Director at Minton's China Works in London Road, Stoke. It is said that Minton held an ambition to make hard-paste porcelain of a quality to match the best products of Sevres. Arnoux's contribution to the Minton company's reputation was many sided. Ironically they abandoned their plans to manufacture hard-paste in favour of the area's traditional bone china composition. In turn Arnoux turned his attention to introducing designs largely based upon early French earthenwares e.g. majolica and Henri deux. In addition to his artistic skills Arnoux was a very experienced ceramic chemist. He also wrote several papers on ceramic design and production.

4.   Leon Victor Solon, born 1872.   Studied at Hanley School of Art and South Kensington. Appointed Art Director and Chief Designer at Mintons 1900-1909. Emigrated to the United States in 1909 and set up as an interior decorator.

5.   Stanley Hind in Pottery Ovens, Fuels and Firing, 1937, described the Moore Campbell kiln as being fired with electricity and 'of a straight single truck type and consisting entirely of cast iron or heat resistant steel'. He goes on to write, 'A recent development (1937) of the Moore Campbell kiln has been the Rotolec kiln, which is of a circular, continuous tray type. Sixteen more Moore,Campbell

or Rotolec kilns have now been built.' This figure suggests that Haggar's claim that the kiln was a failure was true only in the longer term.

6.   Reginald Haggar held the view that the Potteries Museum's rich ceramic collections should, as far as were possible, have been presented almost in their entirety. This traditional approach to museum displays was, and continues to be, out of favour with museum professionals and, indeed, most members of the general public. Modern designers of museum displays place a greater emphasis on a selection of representative items accompanied by the relevant (but not excessive) information.

7.   The Michelin Tyre Company moved into Stoke-on-Trent in 1926. It was welcomed as providing a significant employment alternative to the ceramic industry and coal mining.

8.   Haggar's apparent dismissal of Clarice Cliff as a significant ceramic designer should be judged in the context of the early 1970s. I well remember seeing many examples of her 'Bizarre' range in my role as Keeper of Ceramics at the then Stoke on Trent City Museum and Art Gallery. Until the staging of an exhibition of her work at Brighton Museum in 1972 Clarice Cliff's Art Deco style designs were largely overlooked by design historians and collectors alike. Her reputation provides a good example of someone who can be rediscovered by the attentions of the market for collectables combined with the appearance of publications on her work.

9.   Alfred Meigh's collection of potters' marks and backstamps was acquired by author Geoffrey Godden and used as a basis for his standard work on the subject which came out under the title of *An Encyclopaedia of British Pottery and Porcelain Marks* in 1964.

10. The Schools of Design in Stoke on Trent enjoyed an excellent reputation from their inception in 1845 with many of their students moving on to secure important appointments in Art Education and Industry. With the advent of National Competitions in 1857 they headed the table for the number of students receiving awards.

League Table of medals awarded in 1865:

North Staffordshire Schools (of which there were 4)	100
South Kensington, Male	52
South Kensington, Female	36
Metropolitan, Female	38
Sheffield	37
Birmingham (2 schools)	36
Manchester	34
Glasgow	22

11. Since the closure of John Maddock Ltd, Newcastle Street and Dale Hall, Burslem, the current location of Haggar's panoramic painting is unknown.

12. Saint Paul's Church (built 1828) was, unfortunately, demolished in 1974 and replaced by a smaller, plainer structure. During the course of its demolition numerous examples of Enoch Wood's products were recovered from the building's foundations and retained by the demolition contractor. They included a jasper ware plaque based upon Rubens' painting of 'The Descent from the Cross', portrait busts in basaltes and enamel-painted earthenware, and tablewares printed in underglaze blue. Enoch Wood had a keen sense of history and was a prolific burier of items 'for the gratification of future antiquaries.'

13. At the time of my interview with Reginald Haggar the City's wastelands, to which he refers,

were undergoing a major landscaping project that would see them converted into the 'Forest Park'. Areas that were once dominated by coal tips and slag heaps have been transformed into a landscape of green trees and hills.

14. Gordon Mitchell Forsyth was born 1879 in Fraseburgh, Aberdeenshire; trained in Aberdeen later going on to the Royal College of Art; in 1902 he won a travelling scholarship to Italy: from 1902 to 1905 he was art director to Minton Hollins & Co. before moving on to the Pilkington Tile and Pottery Company in 1906; he was especially acclaimed for his painting on ceramics in the lustre technique; he served as a designer to the Royal Air Force (1916-19) later becoming Superintendent of art instruction at Stoke and Burslem Schools of Art; later became an adviser to the British Pottery Manufacturers Federation. Forsyth's influence on art education in North Staffordshire was considerable.

Harry Tittensor 1888-1942 was a designer of ceramic transfers and a painter. Student at Burslem School of Art 1902-8. Master in Charge, Stoke School of Art 1932-34.

15. Although Reginald Haggar did not reveal details of his salary whilst employed by Minton's as Art Director it was almost certainly, in relative terms, less than the salary paid to Leon Arnoux during his time in the same post. During the period 1848 to the end of the century their artists and designers were amongst the highest paid of any industrial designers in Britain. The following details are from Minton's Salaries Book for the years 1868 and 1882:

		1868	1882:
Leon Arnoux	Art Director	£1,200	£1, 500
Marc Louis Solon	Designer	400	800
Antonin Boullemier	Figure painter	400	205
Paul Comolera	Modeller	210	
John Henk	Modeller	151	
Edmund Reuter	Designer		250
W.H. Foster	Figure painter	275	
Thomas Allen	Figure painter	160	
Thomas Kirkby	Figure painter	156	
Aaron Green	Gilder	117	
Richard Pilsbury	Flower painter	117	
Charles Toft	Ornamenter	104	

16. At the time of our conversation Reginald Haggar was making plans to move to the Isle of Man. This decision was, in part, made as a result of his friendship with the author Richard Adams and his wife Elizabeth.

Artist, author and designer, Reginald Haggar as depicted in his 'self portrait
with black grapes'. This painting marked a difficult period in Mr Haggar's
life following a road accident that seriously injured both himself and Mrs
Haggar. Reginald Haggar is remembered for his distinguished contribution
to the artistic life of North Staffordshire.

Dolby's Mills, 1974.
A Reginald Haggar watercolour of the
Potteries

Leon Arnoux at work in his studio at the
Minton factory. Reginald Haggar took up
a similar role for the company from 1929.
Throughout Arnoux's career with Minton
he was one of the highest paid designers
working in any industry of the period.

Designers and prestige painters were the aristocracy of the ceramic industry, a status reflected in their dress and working environment.

Some manufacturers achieved an international reputation that attracted key workers, especially designers, from the continent. Herbert Minton, right, established a trend with the appointment of Leon Arnoux that was continued by his nephew Colin Minton Campbell. During the 1870s more than twenty artists from France, Germany and Switzerland arrived in North Staffordshire.

Marc Louis Solon, a French-born designer employed by the Minton factory from 1870. Along with several of his contemporaries Solon came to England at this time to avoid conscription for the Franco-Prussian War in 1870. Arnold Wain recalls having experienced the influence of the Solons, both father and son, at the time of his employment by Minton's during the early 1900s.

Solon's best known contribution to the Minton factory's reputation was the introduction of pate-sur-pate during the early 1870s. This elaborately decorated pen and ink stand dates from the mid 1880s. *By kind permission of The Potteries Museum.*

Arnold Wain
Dentist, Lay Preacher
Former City Councillor, Stoke on Trent City Council

Interviewed Stone Road, Trentham, 1974

Arnold Wain was one of the first people to respond, via the local press, for contributors to my project in personal testimony. Although I had, at this point, never met Mr Wain he was known to me as a well-known local dentist and as a result of his political connections with the City Council.

Like the previous contributor his skills as a public speaker made conducting an interview a very straightforward and pleasant experience. Following an initial question he provided what proved to be a fascinating insight into the trials and tribulations of working-class life in Stoke on Trent during the early years of the last century.

Minton's, where he was employed as a boy of thirteen, was then one of the most prestigious and important ceramic manufactories in Europe, especially following its recruitment of artists and designers from the continent, in particular France. Minton's premises were in keeping with this status, Reginald Haggar described them as warranting the description quarter mile Minton.

It is especially ironic that this publication has appeared at a time that has witnessed the removal of Minton, to make way for a Sainsbury's supermarket. Leon Arnoux, also mentioned by Mr Haggar, was one of several designers who came to work for the firm from the late 1840s. There followed a specially significant influx of talent from France with the onset of the Franco -Prussian War in 1870. It was in this year that Marc Louis Solon joined Minton's as a senior designer.

The Solon described in Mr Wain's account was almost certainly Leon Victor, the son of Marc Louis. His reference to the designer's age as being in his thirties does not tally with Solon senior's profile who, at the time of Mr Wain's employment at Minton's, was a man approaching retirement.

What follows describes in almost equal measure the two areas of a career that exceeded fifty years, a phase at Minton followed by his profession as a dentist. The contrast in fortunes represented by the transition from factory boy to dentist could hardly be more dramatic.

The monument of Colin Minton Campbell, erected in 1887, was a recognised meeting place for those looking for a day's work. Arnold Wain describes his father's daily trip to the monument. This photograph was taken on the day of the unveiling ceremony.

Most of Minton's artistic elite resided at The Villas off London Road, Stoke-upon-Trent. Both Arnoux and Solon had homes there.

Arnold Wain

I was born the son of a potter in Stoke. I remember how the chief features of that day were poverty, absolute abject poverty, and unemployment. The pawn shops flourished. Outside every pawnshop at seven o'clock on Monday mornings you'd find a queue of people. I joined them. I was taken as a little boy by my mother to Palfreyman's pawn shop in Stoke, and there we waited for the pawn shop manager to come along and open the shop. In we would troop and put our parcels on the counter, and he would open each one and tell us how much he would allow. We would ask him for five shillings or half a crown, whatever it was, and I've often heard old women beg this man to give them an extra sixpence, just lend them an extra sixpence. "Oh make it another sixpence Ralph" (pronounced Rafe), they used to say, "You know I always fetch ''em out on Saturdays". But very often this was impossible and she'd have to be satisfied with half a crown or three and sixpence. This was quite a feature of that particular time, tremendous unemployment.

Of course the pottery industry has always been one of the worst paid industries in England. Even when I was a young man the top wage that a fully apprenticed potter could earn was thirty shillings a week. Miners got two pounds a week because their work was more dangerous. But that was the standard.

I can remember too in my boyhood, amid this poverty, moonlight flits taking place. People couldn't pay their rent, and so in the middle of the night they would steal away with their bits of furniture to their new address in the hope that the landlord wouldn't find where they'd gone to live. And this was the general picture, it was hunger. When I was a boy at school, at Christmas the boys without any father, or very poor boys, would be given a ticket for a Christmas dinner in the Town Hall at Stoke. This Town Hall now is our Jubilee Hall. The Jubilee Hall was the Town Hall that's what I mean to say, before the King's Hall was built. And it was there that my brothers used to go for the Christmas dinner for poor children. And I remember my mother used to make them a little linen bag, and hang it round their necks under their shirts. As they had their Christmas dinner in the Town Hall, they would put little bits of whatever they were eating at the time into the bag, a little potato, a little bit of vegetable, a little bit of cake, and they would bring the bag home and I would sit with it at the kitchen table picking this out and eating what I could from the present they brought me. The day came when I too went as a poor boy to the Christmas dinner.

It's rather interesting to me to recall that many years later after that the Town Hall had been replaced by the King's Hall, one of the most beautiful halls, I think, in the country. My daughter's, wedding reception was held there, and the Lord Mayor and Lady Mayoress attended because I was a member of the City Council at the time. The wedding ceremony was performed by Bishop Crick, the Bishop of Stafford, who later became Bishop of Chester. This period has very precious memories for me.

There was no relief or very little outdoor relief for the very poor people. I can remember when I was very little, about four years of age, my mother going, with a neighbour, to the relieving officer at Stoke and asking for help. But I can remember now my mother coming back. I can see her now standing in our little kitchen, and saying to the woman who came with her, "Well fancy, we didn't expect to be received like that". They had been told that there was no outdoor relief, not even a loaf of bread but we could all go into the work house, and my mother was laughing with this neighbour saying "We haven't quite come to that !"

Well, my father, who was a sanitary placer, a skilled job, that is one of the most skilled in the clay department of a factory, was offered a foreman's job at Newcastle-on-Tyne. He went there with my mother and they were there for eighteen months. It was a very unhappy time for my mother because father, who'd always been fond of a pint of beer, even as a young man, was drinking fairly heavily at that time, and my mother was very unhappy there. They returned to Stoke but they never got a home together again.

I'm quite sure my father never bought any furniture and we had very scanty fittings in our home, a bed perhaps or a couple of beds and a table and a chair or two, that was all. My first memory is being in the little house in which I was born, behind the present AA offices at the bottom of Hartshill bank. I remember one day being locked in the house with a knocking at the door and a voice outside saying to me "Open the door sonny, we'll give you a penny". Well I couldn't have opened the door, I couldn't have turned the key because I was only a tiny child. But it was the bailiffs. We were in the process of being visited by the bums who were trying to get in to take what bit of furniture we'd got. My mother called, "You must do nothing of the kind". I remember that from that house we did a moonlight flit to another house. The furniture was brought by my brothers on a small hand cart, so you can tell we didn't have much furniture.

Well, I want to speak specially of the potting industry. My father was a potter but he never had a regular job after he was a young man. For some reason or other he would not have the responsibility, and was content to be a labourer, to do an odd job here and there, an odd day's work here and there. He would go out every morning, at six o'clock, to the centre of Stoke, in what we called the Campbell Square then, and would stand by the Campbell Monument.[1] This monument now stands outside the main entrance of the Minton China Works in London Road, Stoke. It then stood in the middle of Campbell Place. It was surrounded by heavy railings and at each corner was a lamp. Any man in those days who wanted a day's work would go there at six o'clock in the morning and stand there. If a foreman potter wanted a man to do a day's drawing, or a day's labouring of any kind he would go to the monument and hire him for the day, and for that the man hired would be paid about five shillings a day. My father always went there, every morning. If no one fetched him for a job he would come back home, and he would sit in the house and read, and then he would go out in the evening and would come back drunk. He always said that it was easier for him to get drink than to get money for a loaf of bread, because people would treat him. His favourite pub still stands, The Staff of Life in Hill Street, Stoke. It was there that he took my staff of life for the first ten to fifteen years of my life.

He never bought me anything. He never bought me a pair of socks or a pair of trousers. He never bought anything, any member of my family anything. He never possessed anything, he was completely possessionless. I never remember him having a penknife or a watch. I was never told, "put that down it's your father's", because my father didn't have anything. Well, I remember that before I started school, and during my early school days, he would do a few days work at Minton's China Works in London Road. It was there that

I went to work when I left school at the age of thirteen. My birthday is in the middle of August and of course the school broke up at the end of July and so although I should have waited until the 22nd of August before I began to work, I began to work at the beginning of August, a fortnight before my thirteenth birthday. I went to work at Minton's in the green house. That sounds rather strange I suppose to many people, to think there is a green house on a factory. But this is the place where the ware is brought in the clay state, immediately it is made. It's brought to the green house on boards, boards about six feet long by one foot wide, and placed in stillages there. Then the placers placed this clay ware in the saggars prior to it being put in the ovens to be fired.

The wares were put in saggars bedded in powder which was called flint. My father's job was sitting up with the ovens at night in order to stoke up, under the supervision of foreman fireman. It was a very exacting operation because there was no means of testing the fire except by very primitive methods, putting in a few small cups, tiny egg cups without handles.[2] These were placed in the oven where they could be reached by long pokers, and they would be tested half way through the firing, which took two or three days to do. Of course when you think that there were hundreds of pounds worth of ware being fired at once it was a very responsible and anxious time.

Another job that my father had, and I tell you this to show you the awful conditions under which pottery operatives worked in those days. We had you remember the great danger of lead poisoning which killed many people every year. This was caused through the lead in the dipping house. The glaze was put on the biscuit ware when it came out of the ovens. The ware was dipped in this liquid then fired in the glossed oven.After that they came out shiny and beautiful as we know them to be. My father's job, or one of his jobs, was to reduce this flint, in which the ware was placed, back to powder. This was because during the firing process it was made hard. It had to be riddled and sieved back into powder form, this was his job. Well, he used to work in a small shop. I should think it would be twelve feet by six, and there were two sieves which were shaking by being mechanically operated. My father would shovel the hard flint into these sieves. You can imagine the dust that would arise. I think there were already then fans of some kind put here and there about the works where the dangerous processes were carried out, but they were quite inefficient. When I wanted to talk to my father it was no good my shouting to him to come out because he couldn't see where he was because of the dust. And so I had to walk in this little place and grope about until I could feel my father and pull him to show that I wanted to talk to him. He would then come out to speak to me. It gives you some idea of the danger of the work. Not one solitary man in my father's team, around the ovens, among the placers and the labourers, was fit. They all had lung trouble, and most of them died, as my father did, of what was called "potters' rot".

I've talked about the poverty of those days, and it was most abject. The poor people found it impossible to get medical treatment. I know they could go to the infirmary as outpatients, but as far as any treatment in their home was concerned or any opportunity of going to a doctor's surgery for treatment, this was not possible unless the parents of children entered the doctor's dispensary for a few coppers a week. There was no provision for any illness of any kind. Why I mention this is because I suffered from malnutrition from the age of twelve until I was twenty one. This took the form of running sores, breakings out, wounds on my left foot and my right arm. On my left foot there were two running wounds which continually discharged pus, all day long. One wound was on top of the foot near to the little toe, and the other wound was on the side of the foot by the same toe. And the wound on the right arm was on the upper, minor side of the arm. These I say continuously drained pus and were a source of pain and distress.

Every morning when I woke up I had to bandage my foot. Well, bandage is rather a swanky term for what actually happened. I began work as I've said at the age of thirteen. I had to be at Minton's works at eight o'clock in the morning. I would come down stairs and the first thing I had to do before I put my stocking on was to cover these discharging wounds. I used to ask my mother if she would give me a piece of rag for this purpose. She would dive into a drawer because I'm sorry to say that my mother, who's mother in turn died before she was twelve years of age, had no idea, not the slightest elementary knowledge of medicine. She hadn't ever heard of boracic powder, or boracic lint or any antiseptic. She had no knowledge whatever of treating any simple ailment. She would hunt in a drawer full of old cloths or pieces of string or any odds and ends, and she would get a rag and tear a strip off and throw it to me across the kitchen and I would wrap my foot in this. Well then followed a very painful experience. I had to cram this swollen, painful foot which was not bathed, except on very rare occasions, and it was always hot and inflamed, and disturbed my nights of course.

When I look back now if only somebody could have provided me with a pair of sandals it would have been a God-send to me, but I'd never heard of sandals, and there was no effort made on the part of my family, and my elder brothers who were then working of course. It meant tears every morning as I tried to get my painful foot into my boot. But as it happened every morning nobody took any notice, it was just part of the ritual of the day. I set off to walk with a bad limp along to Minton's works about a quarter of an hour's walk from where we lived.

Almost every morning my father would come through the backyard gate and walk down the yard to the back door to come into the house. He was on his way home from the Monument. Nobody had hired him, and so he was coming into the house. My mother would say, "What now't again?" And he'd say, "No, nothing now".

"Well", she'd say, "I don't know what we're going to do. I don't know where the next loaf is coming from. I don't know where the rent is coming from". And this conversation went on practically every day of every week. No wonder therefore I never asked the question, "Can I stay at home? My foot's too painful, I can't possibly work on this.". I never once asked that question. The only time I did stay at home was when I had blood poisoning and the red line came up the back of my leg. My knee stiffened and I couldn't possibly walk, and then I had to stay at home. That happened many times between the age of twelve and twenty one.

At twenty-one I had the wounds scraped at the North Staffordshire Infirmary. From then things got better with me. But that is another part of the story.

There are one or two interesting things about my period at Minton's. After I'd worked in the green house for a year, and that was a wonderful opportunity for me to get to know the clay departments, because I worked with two bosses who sent me to all the departments, into the pressing shop, into the casting shop, into the turning shop, into the thrower's department, and so I got a very good idea of potting. After that I went to become an apprentice polisher. This is the department where the ware is taken and every blemish removed from it. If there is a tiny flaw, a tiny speck of dirt that had flown on to it during the process of firing, if in the decorating department, when the gilders and paintresses were decorating the ware, if the tiniest blemish was made on the plate, it had to be removed. You must remember that this was Minton's China Works, one of the finest names in the potting world. The ware made on the china works was the most expensive. A lot of it went to America and it had to be perfect. Women were trained to examine the ware very carefully under powerful lights in order that they might detect any slight fault. The ware was brought into the polishing shop and these faults were removed by wooden wheels or cork wheels, and they were left so that you couldn't see where the fault had been.

During the time I was there I came in touch with Mr Solon, one of the art directors, a Frenchman of some considerable distinction. I can remember him bringing his own particular ware called pate-sur-pate. They were brought into the polishing shop and to my boss who used to polish them. They were very special jobs indeed and caused quite a considerable amount of excitement.

What I remember of Mr Solon, remember I'm talking now of memories that I formed as a boy of thirteen or fourteen. He was a man of about thirty-five years of age I should imagine, of slight build, dark, clean shaven,of a definite French caste and although I never spoke to him or heard him speak he was a figure of great interest to the pottery operatives, if only because he was a Frenchman. I can remember seeing him many times. He lived in The Villas at Stoke, very near to the works, the Minton works that is.[3] I also remember Mr Boullemier who was also in the art department there, a stiff almost fat man.[4]

He again was a man who commanded the attention and respect of a good many of the operatives. He was one of the higher hierarchy.

Frank Morrall was the manager of Minton's in my day and one of the jobs when I first went to work on the factory was that I had to go and see him every morning to see if he wanted me to fetch his lunch from his home in Mount Pleasant, Fenton, which was about a mile and a half from the works. I had to set off at about twelve o'clock and go to his home where I would receive his dinner wrapped in a large red handkerchief. I would be told to run as fast as I could so that it wouldn't be cold by the time I got to the factory. Because of my foot I'm afraid it would be cold by the time I got to Minton's, but there it was. I did that every day for a long time.

I must not dwell too much on this part of my work on the factory because at the age of sixteen, after three years, I left potting because I had an opportunity of going to work with a dentist, a man named Sarsen. He had lived in Rhyl and was, indeed, Welsh. He had practised as a dentist in Rhyl for many years before coming to the Potteries where he had a relative. He started a practice in Church Street Stoke. One of my elder brothers, I had four brothers and one sister, went to him to have a tooth extracted. This man was trying to build up a practice. He was a stranger and was very anxious to make what contacts he could with the local people. He asked my brother if he could help him by trying to get patients for him.

Now, you must be told that dentistry in those days, about 1908-10, was very different from what it is today. Then most dentists were not qualified, they were not hospital trained. Most dentists were trained by other dentists who were in practice in their own town.

And so my brother went to work for Mr Sarsen, and part of his job was to go out to the streets and canvas for patients. Because dentists were allowed to canvas they were allowed to advertise. I must say that I didn't know this of course when I was a boy, but there were two standards of dentists, there was the qualified dentist who had spent many years training, who was trained in dental hospitals, and who had to pass a stiff examination. There were the unregistered dentists who were very often employed by the registered men, and of course for them there was not a problem. As long as they worked for a qualified dentist they were allowed to practice. They could not only make dentures, but they could also operate in his surgery. But if one of these unqualified dentists desired to start in practice on his own, then there was trouble. Not that they did anything illegal, the law of the land allowed these men to practice, but the medical profession were dead against them because they were not qualified. As long as they were with the qualified dentist the doctors did nothing about it but immediately they opened their own surgeries then the doctor's hand was turned against them, and they were very badly treated. They were denounced right, left and centre by the doctors. Now, this came as a tremendous shock to me.

When I first went into dentistry, because I'd been able to help my brother in his work for this dentist, I did a few hours work, and they took a liking to me, they asked my brother if I would work for them. Well, I was working at Minton's factory, therefore in comparison this was a very good move. But the great danger, and the great hindrance to my going to work there was my malnutrition and my bad foot. I didn't walk one step without pain from the age of twelve until I was twenty-one. One of the things I'd got to do if I went into dentistry was to go with my employer when he visited his branches. Now, he not only had his main surgery in Stoke but he had branches at Audley, Halmerend, Bignall End, Chesterton, Butt Lane, Kidsgrove and so on. He'd visit these branches to fit dentures and carry out treatment, and allow people to pay by instalments because, of course, poverty stalked the land. I remember when dentists advertised they used to advertise a set of teeth for a shilling a week. The dentist would go round to the homes of his patients and collect these shillings, and this was part of my job. I would go off with the boss on Monday morning. We would go to Audley, and he would set off in one direction to visit his patients and collect his shillings, and I would go off in another direction and visit other patients and collect the shillings. We would meet at lunch time, at a little shop, and we would have our lunch together. He would then see patients at the chemist's shop at Audley.

This was the great problem, was I going to be able to hold this job down, could I work? I couldn't tell the boss what was wrong with me because of course he wouldn't have employed me. One day when he found me limping as I walked along by his side, he asked me if I was limping and I said, "No", of course. He said "I thought you were limping". I knew that if he knew that I was suffering from a serious disability he wouldn't employ me and I would lose my job. As you might have guessed I fought my way through this and gradually got stronger and better. Because, having left the factory and having learned something about the importance of diet, about which my parents knew nothing, and in any case they couldn't afford a proper diet, I was able, when I went into dentistry, to discover the value of fruit and vegetables. I tackled these things myself, and I became gradually stronger.

When I had my operation at the infirmary, which was a very shocking experience because I was only given a whiff of gas, and I suffered great pain while my wounds were being scraped. I lived in dread of that for many years. The memory of it was a shocking thing. It was a terribly wrong thing to do. It was very wicked thing to treat a patient in that way, and I haven't quite forgiven the infirmary that yet.

Well, there it was. When I went to see Sarsen about this job I was entirely misled. He said to me, "Well Mr Wain when we take a pupil like you, we usually ask a premium of a hundred guineas". I was dumbfounded. A hundred guineas! I'd never seen a hundred pennies all at once in my life, and to be told that I was to be taken into the paradise of paradises, where usually one had to pay a hundred guineas. I was to be taken in free of charge, and paid about seven shillings and sixpence a week. It was absolutely beyond my wildest dreams. As I say, I didn't know that in three or four years I should find out the truth that I should be stigmatised as a quack because I wasn't qualified.

This man told me nothing of this. It came as a tremendous shock to me, and I suffered for that for the first twenty years of my practice. It was terrible to find, unexpectedly, the hand of every doctor, and the hand of every dentist who was qualified, against me. They would do anything they could to turn patients away. I suffered agonies as a result of this treatment because I was a young Christian. I was already preaching. I began to preach in the back streets of Stoke when I was fourteen years of age, and have gone on preaching. I've been a lay preacher of the Church of England for sixty years. I was a young Christian wanting to do my best, and doing my utmost to serve my patients. Of course it was a terrible thing for me to have to suffer this insult, a continuous insult from the medical profession.

Well, I started in practice on my own in Stoke in 1914 and I quickly had among my patients members of the potting industry, some from the factory in which I'd worked came to me as patients. Some of them were very kind about my profession, and congratulated me on having bettered myself by leaving the factory. Others never ceased to remind me of my humble beginnings, and would very pointedly say, "Oh, well of course this is much better than being on a potbank isn't it?" So I received the remarks of different people. You've got to remember that I did all this within a square mile. I've written my autobiography and entitled it *One Square Mile*, because the whole of my life has been spent in one square mile.

To start as a poor boy in Stoke, and to know something of the pawn shops, and the moonlight flits, and the depth of poverty, and then to start in practice as a dentist, was of course a tremendous change, and evoked very different remarks from people who knew me.

Well, there it was, and I gradually built up my practice. We were supplying dentures at a shilling a week. The fee for extractions, when I first started, was a shilling. To have a tooth extracted with a local anaesthetic, cocaine, was a shilling. Cocaine had recently been invented, just before I went into dentistry. Hitherto if anybody in Stoke wanted a tooth extracted they had to go to Nurse Mellor who had a little drug shop in Bath Street, adjoining the library there. She had been at the Infirmary and had this drug store, and anybody who had toothache went to Nurse Mellor and she charged them sixpence. Well, of course, there was no cocaine, it was cold steel. I lived to see the day when Nurse Mellor came in to the surgery where I practised, and stood by the chair, and saw us extract teeth painlessly, and she was amazed.

I gradually built up this practice and went on under the criticism of the medical profession, and the antagonism of the medical profession, until the Dental Act of 1921 was placed on the Statute Book. This registered dentists. All dentists who had been in practice as the sole means of their livelihood for five years were put on the register. Other men who couldn't satisfy that requirement had to pass a medical examination. That altered things and from that day the medical profession looked upon us with kindlier eyes. Up till that time no unregistered dentist could call himself a dentist. We were not allowed to call ourselves dentists or dental surgeons. We could say that we had a dental surgery, we could put a brass plate on our doors and say "Mr A.A Wain, Dental Surgery" but we couldn't call ourselves a dentist.

When the Act of 1921 came about then we could call ourselves dentists. Later on, when a later act came along, we were allowed to call ourselves dental surgeons. So I've seen the progress of dentistry from these beginnings when advertising and canvassing were allowed, to the present state of things when of course no dentist can advertise or canvas or do anything of that kind.

I was preaching as a young lad. I started to preach as I said when I was a little lad of fourteen and I'm now in my eightieth year and I've been a preacher all my life. I've preached in 250 churches and chapels, only six of which are outside the city of Stoke-on-Trent. It has been a very wonderful experience. I'm happy to think in my old age that I've not severed myself from the pottery industry entirely because on most Sundays I am preaching to potters. Most of my congregations are pottery people, and so I still retain my ties with the old factory days at Minton's.

I have much to be thankful for. One of the things that fills my heart with great thankfulness is that my son, John was able to go to Oxford entirely at my own expense. We had no grant from any authority, I paid the whole of his university expenses, and he is now Professor of Poetry at the University of Oxford.[5] This for me is a great source of joy. As my life works out to its concluding stages I am very, very thankful indeed.

Notes

1. It was customary for those out of work, and seeking employment, to stand every morning by a local landmark where they would wait to be recruited for a day's work by a representative of a manufacturer in the area. In the town of Stoke the main landmark for this purpose was the portrait monument of Colin Minton Campbell. In Mr. Wain's father's time it stood in the town centre. At a later date the monument was moved to the forecourt of Minton's factory. Following the recent clearance of the site, to make way for a Sainsbury supermarket, Minton Campbell was disturbed yet again and relocated adjacent to London Road.

2. The firing of ceramics has traditionally been regarded as the most unpredictable stage of the production process. Since a very early period potters have used test or trial pieces of various kinds

that they were able to retrieve at key stages in the firing cycle. Technicians on the continent were, by the end of the 19th century, attempting to systematise pyrometry via the introduction of what were termed 'cones'. A leading figure in these experiments was the German chemist, Hermann Seger. As these cones were not readily available in Britain until the 1930s various cruder alternatives were still being used up until the Second World War period. Mr. Wain's reference to egg cup like test pieces is totally in keeping with this evidence.

3.   The Villas, referred to in this interview, have survived to the present day. Designed in an Italianate style their characteristics would have held an immediate appeal for most artistically sensitive people from the continent. As a result of the Franco Prussian War of 1870 several artists and designers followed Arnoux's example and migrated to North Staffordshire. Most of them moved into The Villas, Arnoux and Solon setting a trend that others chose to follow. The Villas are situated at a right angle to London Road, a little further than a quarter of a mile from the site of Minton's Works.

4. Antonin Boullemier 1840-1900
Worked as a porcelain painter at Sevres until his move to England in 1870 at the invitation of Colin Minton Campbell. Many of his enamelled patterns are based upon paintings by Boucher and Fragonard.

A parian reproduction of the Minton Campbell monument was often given as a retirement award - paternalism personified!

5. John Wain, son of Arnold Wain, became an important literary figure in the second half of the 20th century. He was Professor of Poetry at Oxford 1973-1978 and had a considerable output of work including fiction, poetry, plays and literary criticism. His fiction earned him the title of 'the new Arnold Bennett' because he was the first major novelist to emerge from the Potteries since Bennett. He was awarded the Whitbread Prize in 1982 for his novel *Young Shoulders*. He has written a major work on Arnold Bennett and he has appeared on television many times as an art critic.

The pawnbroker was an important institution in 19th and early 20th century life.

Mr. Spurgeon Tildsley
Pawnbroker, Tildsley's Pawnbrokers,
Marsh Street, Hanley, Stoke on Trent

Interviewed Baddeley Green, 1975.

My interview with Mr Tildsley resulted from a report in the local press that his family's pawnbroking business was scheduled to close in the summer of 1975. Their premises in Marsh Street, Hanley, opposite what is now a Tesco supermarket, was an important part of the business community, in most cases family-owned concerns that had served the local population with varying degrees of commercial success since the 19th century. To name but a few there was Major Stringer's New Hall Porcelain Company, originally situated on the aforementioned Tesco site, Boyce Adams grocers, Swinnerton's caterers, Ridgway's music shop all located in Piccadilly, and at the top end of the town Bratt and Dyke, Huntbach's and Sherwin's music shop.

Smaller concerns of the period included Mr Nagington, a photographer operating from premises in Hope Street, and at the top of the same street the rather object-crowded and dark 'antique shop' of Miss James. Catering perhaps for a slightly higher strata of the collectors' market was the shop operated by the father and son business of Steadman's, again in Piccadilly. Bibliophiles and anyone looking for a book bargain would, in those days, have gravitated to Sanderson's Antiquarian Bookshop.

The decision to include the interview with Mr Tildsley was inevitable given the fact that almost all of those who contributed to my exercise in oral testimony were at least very conscious of, even if they had never had reason to draw on, the pawnbroker's services. Social commentators in the 19th century, in particular the government inspector Samuel Scriven, make frequent references to the endemic poverty that prevailed in all the industrial centres of Britain. In his investigation, conducted during the 1840s in the potbanks of North Staffordshire, he spoke to many who had experienced the need to pawn their possessions, ranging in value from, for example, a well-worn waistcoat to a watch, perhaps handed down by a father or grandfather.

Towards the end of his testimony Mr Tildsley mentions a decline in demand as a reason for his decision to close. His prophesy concerning the future role of pawnbroking was, however, somewhat overturned in the mid 1980s.

PAWNBROKERS.

Bickley, T., Piccadilly
Bickley, Thos., 13, High-street
Blackwood, Jno., 39, Parliament-row

Chawner, Geo., 74, Hope-street
Gommersall, Horace, 99, Broad-street
Harrison, A. J., 148, Leek-road
Harrison, A. J., 53, Palmerston-street
Kent, A., 167, Etruria-road
Kent, Robt., 16, Clarke-street
Knox, A., 11, Bucknall New-rd.
Moore, A., 15, Hulton-street
Palfreyman Bros., 21, Broad-st.; 3, Crown-st., and Bucknall New-road
Powis, J., 104a & 106, High-street
Thompson, G., 39, Trinity-street
Tildsley, H., 147, Marsh-street
Warrilow, Wm., 1, Bold-street, Northwood; & Stafford-street
Warrilow, Wm., 24, Lamb-street

Spurgeon Tildsley outside the shop c.1970.

Left: From the Hanley section of *The Potteries Directory* 1912, under Pawnbrokers.

Mr. Tildsley

When I first went into pawnbroking I was seven years of age. I used to go to the shop at five in a morning and work until half past eight (am), and write a hundred and fifty pawn tickets between 5am and 8.30am. I used to run home, get my breakfast, and go to school. When I came out of school at four o clock I was down the shop at half past four and wrote another hundred and fifty before we closed at ten.

That was in the ordinary days. I got that used to writing that I left school at the age of eleven. I'd passed every standard at the age of eleven.

One of my first tasks was to throw bundles down a chute for them to catch when they came out to give to customers. In 1897, I think it was, we had £1780 worth fetched out of pledge. The money that we took had to be collected by two police officers and taken by wheel barrow to the police station at the town hall. They saved it for us until we opened again on the Monday morning.

We were Butters and Tildsley in those days. In our shop there was a big safe that you could walk into. I remember them fitting it, it was a monster. What they did was this when they fetched it - I was there with Dad - and Dad said to these fellows that had fitted it up, "That'll do, they'll never get in, they can't break through that". The man who'd fitted it said "Do you think so Mr Tildsley." Dad said "Yes they'll never get in that because I shall keep the key safe". The man said, "Well I'll show you something. Have you got a hairpin on you?" Dad gave him a hairpin. The man said, "Now you keep the keys in your pocket", and he just bent the pin put it in the lock, did that, and he was inside it in less than two minutes.

We used to take everything in, organs, pianos, mirrors, prams, we took everything in pledge. I shall never forget they wouldn't allow us electric light, in fact there was no electric light in those days. We had oil lamps to go and find the parcels when they were upstairs. I shall never forget one lad. We'd had a burglary the week before. It was a long room, perhaps as long as from here to those houses across the road (Mr Tildsley was pointing to houses that were some fifty feet away) and he was walking up the stairs when he saw somebody walking towards him, and he got his lamp and threw it at this chap, as he thought, who was walking towards him, but it wasn't a man who was walking towards him, it was himself reflected in a big mirror that was in pledge. The lamp went straight through the mirror.

G.W.E. These big items that you have mentioned, the organs, pianos and things, how did people get them to the shop?

Mr T.   Oh, they brought 'em up with a horse and snoddy. I don't know whether you know pawnbroking much but you see all the tickets had to be kept, and every one that was fetched out we strung with a packing needle, long strings of nothing only tickets for everything that was fetched out.

When we had the first income tax you had to get an accountant to do your returns. All the years before that we had done our own returns. I shall never forget. I didn't go down with Dad but Dad went down himself, and the authorities said, "We can't accept your returns any more - you'll have to get an accountant". Dad said "I've already done them". Alright they said, "Bring your books down and we'll examine them and if we can pass 'em this year we'll let you off and you'll have to get an accountant next year". We had to get a horse and float, a four wheel float, and we packed all the tickets on, one thousand tickets a week for fifty-two weeks. They were all strung up so you can tell how many that was. The cart was loaded up.

I went down with Dad to help him keep the things on the cart. We went down to the income tax people, and Dad walked up with his little book that he'd got all his returns in. They said, "We can't do it simply with the book we want to see all your pledge tickets". Dad said, "You can see them I've brought them all down to you". The man said, "Will you bring 'em up?" Dad said, "No, we can't bring them up they're on a cart outside". The inspector came down and had a look at them and said, "What all of them?" He said, "Ok, we'll reckon that at a thousand a week is fifty two thousand tickets". He said, "Go on then we'll let you off this year, you'll have to get an accountant next year."

G.W.E. Did you in fact do that?
Mr T.   Oh yes.
We used to have chaps come in, they'd pledge a violin and on Saturday night they used to come in. They'd say, "Henry", they called him Henry, "Henry, lend us me violin for an hour, I've no money to fetch it out but I'll bring it back safely". Dad used to lend "em the violin they'd pledged. It was their violin, they'd pledged it you see. They'd go into a pub up the road and they'd play for an hour and make collections. They generally made enough to pay for the violin out, which they didn't want, so they left it in. They made enough to live on for a week in one night, just playing the violin.

At the age of, what should I be, fourteen, I vowed I would never touch drink as long as I live. I never have done, never touched a spot of it, because of a man who came in, I shall never forget it. He said, "I've got five tickets here, one for me overcoat, one for me shoes, one for me trousers, one for me shirt and something else which I can't remember." Dad gave me the five tickets. He said find these parcels for the gentleman. So I found the parcels and put them on the counter. Dad took the tickets off him, took the money from him, and said to me, "Parcel them and tie them with string".

As he was going out of the shop he turned round and said, "Henry aren't I a bloody fool? I've just used all my wages to fetch these things out, and I've got to pledge all of "em back next week to live on." He said, "How can I get out of it?" Dad said to him, "Look, what you pledge for ten bob this week, pledge it for nine shillings next week, and starve yourself for a shilling. In so many weeks you'll have the lot for nothing".

He replied, "Ar conner do that, ar want a drink".

I said to myself here's a man of thirty to forty years of age and he hasn't got the courage of his own convictions to save himself; I'll never drink; I'll never do anything like that as long as I live; and I never have.

G.W.E. In those days drink was a major social problem - possibly one of the main reasons why people brought things to you?
Mr T.   Oh yes, but you see people had no dole, nothing. They used to use every trick imaginable to get money. I've seen the time when Scotch drapers used to come round - this was in the very olden days, before the First World War. They'd come down and they'd go

to a row of houses a few streets below the shop - they're knocked down now. They'd go to the first house and then all the others and say, "Do you want a pair of blankets for a shilling down and a shilling a week, until you've paid for "em?" We've taken as many as thirty pairs of blankets in pledge that same day, that had all come from houses all the way down the street.

G.W.E. What proportion of the things pledged were actually left with you to dispose of?
Mr T.   Oh, quite a few. If you took, we'll say a thousand in, you'd perhaps have a hundred left. Well there were all these people that had had them on tick.

   Also we'd have people come in with a parcel or a shoe box. You've perhaps taken in a pair of shoes off them for four or five weeks, and they'd come in and put "em on the counter and say, "same again Mr Tildsley". Dad'd just push the parcel up without checking inside and say, "Make the ticket out for seven and sixpence for these shoes".

   If any boxes or parcels were left in we used to open them to see why. Sometimes we'd open a box and find that instead of shoes there'd be a brick in it - and they'd pledged it for seven and six. Another time they'd put an old pair of shoes in with holes through the soles and kept the good ones out and they'd got seven and six.

G.W.E. So you didn't always check the goods when they were brought in?
Mr T.   No, you couldn't take in a hundred and fifty pledges in an hour and check every one. You used to take it for granted. Ninety per cent were good, its just the few dishonest people that you got.

G.W.E. What were the strangest things brought in to you?
Mr T.   Bagpipes, and a ship's sextant. Oh we've had nearly everything, silver cups, but the majority was just ordinary clothing goods then but we've had these things like clocks, all sorts of clocks.

   We used to take in a lot of the Lachinel concertinas, and lend them seven and sixpence a piece on them. There was plenty about, we d get perhaps as many as eight or nine in a week. Oh yes we've taken in practically everything.

G.W.E. Were most of your clients working-class people?
Mr T.   Yes, most of "em. Today (we finished last June, 1975) we surrendered the pawnbroker's licence. The shop has been in existence since 1870. We surrendered it because we only took thirty-two pledges in eight months, which wasn't worth bothering with, and the pledges we got were not generally coming from people in poor circumstances as they were in the olden days when people had nothing. If they were out of work they'd starve unless they could find something to pledge or borrow off somebody.

   Today no one can realise what poor people went through in those days. If your husband was out of work, and there wasn't a penny coming in, you'd got to live for a week. Now, how could they live for a week on nothing? They had to use all sorts of means to get a few coppers, and that's how they used to live. It was a terrible life.

G.W.E. Was there a period when your business was used by the city's population more than any other?

Mr T.   No, because there were so many pawnbrokers, thirty-eight in the district, and of course they all took a certain amount in. Ours was the community around us that we took from. But of course you did get occasional people that had come from different places where there wasn't pawnbrokers. We took in from Stafford for a long time, off a feller, Georgian spoons and Georgian silver. He used to pledge ''em for ten pound, and fetch ''em out after three months.

The latest pawnbroking we've done was all by what I'd call wealthy people; it wasn't the poor. People that had their cheque once a month and spent it in the first three weeks and they'd pledge either a gold bangle or something for ten pound to last ''em for the fourth week. Like the poor people they had to put ten pound out of their next month's salary to fetch out what they'd put in for the last month, consequently they never got over it.

G.W.E. So, in recent years it appears that fewer people have had the need to draw on your services? There must have been a time in the past when you did a considerable amount of business, more than you have done in recent times?
Mr T.   Since the 1930s, when they brought dole in and all that stuff, our business dropped you see, from taking a thousand pledges a week, we'd drop perhaps to two to three hundreds. It was taken in mostly from people who were going to work, they wanted a drink and had spent their money. That's why we opened early in a morning, pubs opened early. People would be going to work and they'd pledge just to have a drink on their way to work.

G.W.E. With the drop in trade for objects being pawned did you actually buy things off people ?
Mr T.   You couldn't, it was illegal. There are 164 clauses in the pawnbroker's charter.

G.W.E. So you were never second-hand dealers as such?
Mr T.   We were, but you couldn't buy. The law is such a funny thing and tricky unless you know it. You see if somebody came into the shop and said "lend me five pounds on this", and we said "no we can't afford to lend you five pounds, we'll lend you two", and you said to me "will you buy it off me for three?" we daren't, it's illegal. Once they've offered it for pawn it's illegal for a pawnbroker to buy it.

G.W.E. But if someone came in and made it clear in the first place that they wanted to sell it, what then?
Mr T.   We could buy it, always providing they didn't ask first to pawn it.

I've had some wonderful tussles with people. I remember a lady who pledged two articles, both for five pounds, who went to live in Sunderland. She wrote and said she had lost the tickets but she sent me the money to have them fetched out. I had to return to her the money and say we could do nothing without the ticket. The law of pawnbroking is this: whoever owns the ticket is the owner of the goods, not the person that pledged them. If you pledged an article and you dropped your ticket in the street anybody could fetch it out who picked up the ticket and you couldn't stop them. Whoever owns that ticket is the owner of the goods.

Now, she went to a solicitor in Sunderland and he wrote that if we didn't send her the two parcels he would prosecute. I got on the phone to him and said "prosecute" and he said,

"What do you mean?" I said "prosecute". I said "do you know pawnbroking?" He said, "no". I said well tell that lady if she hasn't got the tickets she has no right to those articles. I said, those articles belong to the person that holds those tickets. When he'd finished he thanked me. He didn't realise there was so much behind pawnbroking.

Why the rule was brought in was this: a chap would come in and say, "Pledge me me watch for a pound". He'd go out, go into a pub for a drink, spend the pound, and he'd say, "Anyone want to buy a ticket for a watch for ten bob"? He'd sell it to somebody for ten bob. Now then he'd come to the shop and say he wanted his watch out but we couldn't let him have it without the ticket because whoever held that ticket was the owner of that watch. The only way he could get it was to get an affidavit, which we could make him out. He'd have to lie and say he'd lost it, and he'd have to go up to the Town Hall to get it signed by a magistrate to promise what he said was true.

G.W.E. Did you have a standard rate amongst pawnbrokers, a rate of interest that is, for money you loaned out?
Mr T.   Oh yes, five pence in the pound, it's never been increased. Right from the start in 1870; it's always been five pence in the pound.

G.W.E.   Did you ever have anyone bring something to you without the knowledge of their opposite number in the case of a man and wife? Were there ever any disputes of this sort?
Mr T.   Very often. We used to get them almost every day, chaps pinching something out of the house and their wife coming up and playing Hamlet.

G.W.E. What generally happened in such cases?
Mr T.   Oh you could do nothing. He'd pledged it, it was only between the man and wife who could fall out at home over it.

G.W.E. What was the period that you allowed anyone to go without actually coming in for an object?
Mr T.   Originally twelve months, but it was reduced to six months. So if you pledged an article in January you could fetch it out until July. If it wasn't fetched out in seven days after the six months it became our property and we could sell it.

G.W.E. What happened in the case of more valuable items?
Mr T.   If it was higher than two pounds it had to go to an auction sale in London. We've just finished up now and sent the lot this June.

G.W.E. So you couldn't have put it into a local saleroom?
Mr T.   No, no, you can't sell it, it's got to be sent to an auction room in London.

G.W.E. Any particular one?
Mr T.   No, but Darell Lloyd was our particular room at Putney Bridge. There was only a few that were sent down this last time, perhaps eight or nine articles. They've just sent us a cheque for £143, that's us out. Now we've nothing in the shop.
G.W.E. You told me earlier that you remember the days when your father used to actually issue soup to people?

Mr T.   Well, you see, before dole or any insurance, when they'd pledged everything they'd got in the house, even the alarm clock off the bedside and the pillow slips, sheets, blankets, and things like that, they'd pledged the lot, they'd come up and say to Dad, "We've nothing left we can pledge, what can you do for us"?

He'd send us lads for perhaps a shilling's worth of bones from the butchers in Stafford Street. You know those washing cauldrons, we'd put the bones in and get two to three pounds of peas, we'd put them in it with an onion and slice it up, mix it all up. We'd then put a fire underneath and boil it. We'd invite customers to come up and we'd give them a bowlful each just to help them a bit.

G.W.E. When did you first open your premises in Marsh Street, Hanley?
Mr T.   We moved in in 1901, and the reason we moved in was this. Charlie Butters died in 1891, left Dad as the other partner. Charlie Butters had three sons and Dad had to pay them as much as he could afford out of the profit each week. The time came when he was not making enough to continue the partnership so it was dissolved.

G.W.E. Coming up to the present do you feel sorry to be closing the business?
Mr T.   I shall miss it more than anything in my life. From the age of seven to the age of eighty-five I've never been out of work. I've never been content to stop at home and I've never been away from the shop, only for holidays. I've never had an illness and I've gone all through that life and never been away from business. To chuck it up like that you can't help but have regrets.

G.W.E. So you might say it represents the end of an era?
Mr T.   The only place that pawnbroking exists, profitably, is at the seaside, not ordinary pleasure resorts but seaports like Liverpool, any port where sailors come in. But in a place like this no, never.

A photograph of Gomersall's, another Hanley pawnbroker .

George Myatt
Thrower
Interviewed Stoke upon Trent, 1974.

At my first meeting with George Myatt I was impressed by the obvious passion he conveyed for his work as a thrower. If proof were needed that certain jobs in the industry promised rewards beyond mere pecuniary considerations, I had the evidence in Mr Myatt's testimony.

At the beginning of our conversation he says that there are no more than some half dozen throwers in Britain. This statement calls for careful qualification. It was certainly true that in the 1970s there were very few throwers working in the factories of Stoke-on-Trent. However, in the wider field of art education, and amongst the Studio Pottery fraternity, throwing was still widely practised. Before my meeting with Mr Myatt I was unaware that he was subconsciously known to me via the existence of a photograph taken on the Longton factory of John Lockett in 1932. Other photographs taken at the same time provide a fascinating record of stages in the manufacturing process underlying the production of a range of wares from pestles and mortars to hospital and chemist's vessels. This pictorial evidence had been handed over temporarily to Hanley Museum, along with the gift of several other items, as a result of the factory's closure to make way for a proposed bus station. Lockett's was probably unique at the time of my visit there in the late 1950s. Its quaint characteristics, including the workshop layout, equipment and products were more in keeping with the 19th century. For example, Mr Myatt mentions that his workshop was once a room that was part of The British Volunteer pub, with other parts of the factory made up from a row of terraced cottages. For anyone witnessing the facilities at Lockett's it would have been readily apparent the construction of Wedgwood's well ordered factory at Etruria in 1769 was in no sense a prototype for other manufacturers to emulate.

Mr Myatt's career was probably unusual in that during a particularly difficult period in the late 1920s/early 1930s he worked for five different employers in the course of a working week. It is, nevertheless, very clear that he had a specially high regard for the Hancock family who owned Lockett's at the time of its enforced closure in 1959. This particular employer-employee relationship provides an appropriate example of the benefits often conferred by a paternalistic management structure. In reading the transcript of my interview with Mr Myatt it is readily apparent that the respect he had for his employer was reciprocated.

The photograph that shows George Myatt, assisted by his wife, includes a selection of profiles displayed on the rear wall of his workshop. There can be no better example of the range of profiles required by a thrower producing a wide variety of products. He describes how they were made using, for example, plate fragments and slate.

In keeping with his status Mr Myatt was well paid with reference to standards of the day. His testimony also provides an interesting description of a system where sub contract labour was commonplace. His wife assistant, for instance, and anyone else who was part of his small team were first and foremost responsible to him, and indeed paid by him, and not directly by the factory owner.

George Myatt and assistant (his wife) in 1932 at John Lockett's factory in Longton.

The management team at John Lockett. The calendar pinned to the office wall for 1932
dates all the photographs in this particular series.

George Myatt

Having been asked to comment on my trade as a potter I must say that conditions before the 1914 War were very different from what they are today, prices were shocking, and as an indentured apprentice I had to make 66 dozen articles for a shilling. I was bound apprentice at W.T. Copeland of Stoke at the glorious figure of five shillings per week for the first six months, then piece work. From then on I had the "Irishman's rise", never earning more than 4/6d until I joined the forces in 1915. After the War I went to work for John Lockett & Co., of Longton as a mortar thrower in 1919. With this job I also worked at George Jones's, doing three days at each place. I was making 56lb. mortars at Lockett's and 2oz. egg cups at Jones's.

During the Depression of 1929 I worked all over the Potteries, at Cauldon Place making honey pots, Wilshaw and Robinson's making tobacco jars, jasper at William Adams's of Tunstall. It was hard work working at all these firms. Some weeks I worked at as many as five different firms. Later I went full-time at John Lockett's again, making big ware such as 56lb. mortars, three gallon barrel jugs, and 14lb. jars. In 1955 Lockett's temporarily closed down so I did one year at Dudson's of Hanley, after which I went to Josiah Wedgwood of Barlaston. I remained there until the age of retirement at the age of seventy-one and a half. I had worked for 58 years in the industry.

My wife also worked for 46 years in the pottery trade, making 104 years between us. Neither of us get a penny pension. I loved my job, and although I have worked at all these firms I can honestly say that I have never had a bad boss, and I never had the sack. Although most pottery workers wages were poor I am sure that we were more content than the operatives of today. Another observation of the industry I have is that eighty per cent of the silicosis today, in my opinion, is caused by too many working in one shop, each making dust for the other. Turners in particular should be in a shop on their own.

In the very old days, between 1910 and 1914, although wages were poor we had to pay for gas, which cost as I remember a penny a week. The gas then was not incandescent, it was just mere flame. We had to pay a penny for that, and a penny a week for someone to sweep the shops.

Up to this point Mr Myatt read out a previously prepared statement that he had written following my initial visit to his home several days earlier. At our first meeting he explained that he felt unable to give me an off the cuff interview. However, what follows was not in any way scripted or delivered with recourse to notes. It is important to mention that in fact he was not aware of my decision to leave the tape running, which I replayed to him at the end of our conversation.

Ironically, he was happier with that part of his interview that was not previously prepared. The belief that what he was saying was off the record had a relaxing effect on his contribution.

G.W.E. You mentioned working at a factory that I visited in the late 1950s, namely John Lockett's of Longton. Can you tell me something about its layout as you remember it, and the conditions there?

G.M.   I can. Lockett's was a conglomeration of small houses. It was my favourite firm. It employed between fifty and sixty operatives, and we had an exceptionally good boss, Mr William Hancock. He was a real gentleman.

G.W.E. Was he a master potter in the old sense. In other words was he fully conversant with the whole pottery-making process?

G.M.   Yes, he was a complete master potter who knew every job and how it should be done.

G.W.E. You say that the factory was made up from several terraced cottages. I have been told by other people I have interviewed that this was not uncommon at one time.

G.M.   The shop that I worked in was two little cottages with the centre wall knocked out. It made an ideal shop for me. I always worked in my own shop. Where we made boxes, where the boxmaker worked, that was an old pub, The British Volunteer in King Street. It was a beautiful shop and had 'The British Volunteer' etched in the window, and the original tile floor was still there. Almost everyone, the pressers, the casters worked in another little cottage, and there was a square in the centre where we used to go and get water from a tap. It was really a lovely firm by today's standards - it was a smile to most people, but to my way of thinking it was the best firm in North Staffordshire.

G.W.E. So what did you make at Lockett's?

G.M.   All hospital requirements, anything from sick-feeders, water bottles, mortars, pestles, chemist's jars in blue and pink that you sometimes see displayed in chemist's shops. They had canopy covers and dome covers. They were a really good article at the time.

G.W.E. You explained that mortars were wheel thrown, but how did you make pestles?

G.M.   The same. They didn't pug'em or anything like that. You made the pestles with the mortars. In the early days they used to make a solid lump of clay for a pestle that they later turned both top and bottom. The screw was put in and then the thick part of the pestle was nosed off at the bottom. Later the turner would run his pestle onto a spindle, and that saved him from putting it on twice. The screw you see made it far cheaper because it halved the cost of turning a pestle. But mortars, through being thick, were more tricky. You were a good mortar thrower if they didn't crack. That was the art of making mortars. The loss from cracking mortars could be terrific.

G.W.E. How many did you lose before they were fired?

G.M.   Well, there were so many dodges with mortars. They could crack round the groove, the bottom, across the bottom, through them being a couple of thicknesses. The bottom and the sides were not so thick. In drying the pull used to crack them on the bottom. I've known ninety-nine out of a hundred crack, and I've known a hundred out of a hundred good. If you got a hundred per cent you could consider yourself a top notch mortar thrower.

G.W.E. Were you paid by the piece - piecework?

G.M.   Well, originally I was but I'd had enough piece work before I went into the army in 1915. I've never been a piece work thrower since but I always was a top price thrower.

G.W.E So the mortars that say cracked in drying were not a direct loss to you?
G.M.   No, they were a loss to the firm. That's why, although I say it myself, the boss was a toff to me because I think I was a toff to him for producing a good article.

G.W.E. In addition to mortars you made general hospital and laboratory wares. Lockett's never made tablewares then?
G.M.   No I think that it was the downfall of John Lockett. You see at one time the box trade used to be a terrific affair, fish paste, anchovy paste, toothpaste, all used to go in little boxes. Well, when Pond's vanishing cream, for instance, was put in glass jars they lost the order. They were earthenware before, and when the scarcity came about, after the War, the meat paste, and anchovy paste, which was put in hot, started to be put in glass jars. John Lockett, being a little, private, family firm never seemed to go in for anything else. Their trade gradually dwindled down. As they lost an order it was as if they never bothered to replace it.

G.W.E. I am familiar with the meat and toothpaste jars. Many of them are probably not as old as they look. So what you are telling me is very interesting because it suggests that these jars were being made until fairly recent times. When did you last throw these items?
G.M.   Fish and meat paste jars were being made until we'll say twelve months after the 1939-45 War started, and they started rationing. It was when rationing came in that they started putting anchovy paste and meat paste in glass jars. Rationing killed the trade never to come back.

G.W.E. Did Lockett's apply the transfer-printed labels to the lids of jars?
G.M.   All the print, everything. They were ready for filling up when they went from Lockett's.

G.W.E. You have previously mentioned being the exception to the low wages usually paid to pottery workers.
G.M.   I was always well paid after my apprenticeship.

G.W.E. Can you tell me more about that. How much were you paid just after the First World War?
G.M.   Well, as I told you previously, before the War, that is the 1914-18 War, I never took my mother less than six shillings a week. After the War I expected more, and that's the reason I went to Lockett's. Mr Hancock, he was so fair with me, he said, "How much a day do you want George?" I said, "Well, I've no idea sir." I had no idea what the wages were. He said, "Well, the feller you are going to follow has left his settling book in that cupboard." He said "He got 12/6d. a day, pre-war." (That made it 21/3d, in 1920.) "When you can do what he did I'll give you his wages."

That was twenty-five shillings a day, and twenty-five shillings for Saturday mornings. I got seven pound ten a week in 1921 at John Lockett, and I've never worked for a penny less at any other firm since.

G.W.E. Judging by what other people have told me that was substantially above the average paid to pottery workers at that period.

G.M.   Other people? Well, a turner only got half as much as a thrower. You see where throwers have slipped up since, or at least been overtaken by machine methods, the Potters' Union stuck up for turners but never got throwers a penny rise this last fifty years. They even had departmental rises where turners got twenty shillings a week on top of their pay. This was in the early thirties, but throwers got nothing. A thrower has had to get his own wages, he's had to negotiate his own because the union has never been any use at all to a thrower, an earthenware thrower at least. I'm only speaking as an earthenware thrower. It may be different with china. The union never lifted a hand to help an earthenware thrower.[1]

G.W.E. How many throwers did they employ at Lockett's during your time there?

G.M.   Only two throwers on Lockett's. There had once been three. I was head thrower for thirty-five years. When I worked at Copeland there was six, and when I worked at Wedgwood's there was about eight. Today, I think there's only about four or five throwers in England.

G.W.E. When you went into the industry, did you say in 1910, was it ever suggested that you might consider going into some other trade or was there no other option for you?

G.M.   No. When I first went in in 1910 my brother was a thrower at Copeland's, and he got me to go as a turner. Well, I found out that a turner, pre-war, would get thirty shillings a week. Throwers were getting three pounds, the journeyman throwers that was. So I wasn't going to go in for turning. I happened to get indentured and went apprentice, I think it would have been early 1911, and as a thrower. Money was the reason I went for throwing. Since then I've never wanted to do anything else because the creative part of throwing made your job interesting and satisfying. I've always been pleased with my own job, and would have refused any promotion.

G.W.E. In Hanley Museum we have some photographs taken on John Lockett in about 1933, the interesting point being that you appear on one of them.

G.M.   That was me.

G.W.E. The photograph shows you sitting in front of a wall on which are hanging profiles and ribs. How were these used?

G.M.   Well, you see, I could tell you quite a lot about ribs. The rib is a piece of slate, school slates were always the best, made to represent the inside of the article. They were filed exactly to shape the inside of the article, and the thrower held the rib in his left hand and made it smooth inside. The thrower finished the inside of the article, and the turner shaped the outside. The rib made it that the inside was finished.

G.W.E. Did you make your own ribs?

G.M.   Yes, we all made our own ribs because ribs are like pens. It's very rare that you can use another man's ribs, very rare.

G.W.E. Is this why so many were inscribed with the thrower's, or at least, maker's name?

G.M.   Yes, you will find some of mine and some that I left at Wedgwood that have got my name on them.

G.W.E. Was this so that other people wouldn't take them?
G.M.   It was just that you liked to think that if you had a good rib you'd put your name on it. There was one glorious rib that I had at Lockett's. It was one of very few ribs that I could use straight away, and it had been made by a man name Jess Amison. On the back of it said "William so and so, born so and so, died so and so. He was a good and generous master."

G.W.E. So you actually used that rib for your throwing at Wedgwood's?
G.M.   I did and it's at Wedgwood's now. I wish I'd never left it there.

G.W.E. So what was the usual number of ribs for a thrower to have?
G.M.   You had a rib for everything you made. I'd got hundreds. You'll find that at the back of that picture there's a wall of 'em. You'd got everything egg cups, vases, mortars, every mortal thing that you made, you had a rib for it.

G.W.E. Were the slate ribs preferred to ribs in pottery? I mention this because some that I have seen were actually made from fragments of plates.
G.M.   That was before they had any kind of refined slate. They'd even make them from roofing tiles at one time. I had quite a few of those made of earthenware. Yes, quite a lot in the early 19th century were made of earthenware. They were plates that had been trimmed off and made perfect. You had to soak them before they could be used otherwise they stuck to the clay as it went round.

G.W.E. What about the wheel you threw on? I understand that in the old days you had a very good wheel at Lockett's, an old string wheel.
G.M.   At Copeland's I worked off steam, and when I went to Lockett's in 1919 I worked on a string wheel. I'd never seen one before, a beautiful string wheel.[2] I should say it was the best in the country, never should have been destroyed. I worked off that wheel from 1919 until about 1941, it may have been 1942. Before I had an electric motor I can safely say that the old fashioned string wheel, if you had a good woman wheel turner, was the best method of throwing. It helped you quite a lot. You could keep both your feet firm whereas with a motor, steam or electric, you had a treadle - you were a one-legged thrower kind of style. Lockett's string wheel, the one that I worked off, was the last in existence. I think I was probably the last man in this country to earn his living on a string wheel.

G.W.E. What date would that be?
G.M.   About 1941, during the War. We had an electric motor at Lockett's. It was their first motor. I told the boss if he'd buy me a motor I'd buy him one, and I did. It was an expensive job, throwing was, when they had a string wheel I had a wheel turner, a woman, a taker off, and a looker to the ware. If my wages were seven pounds ten my bill was fifteen pounds. The man got half my wages and the woman got a quarter. So my wage bill was doubled. Lockett's never begrudged that at all. They were a wonderful family were the Hancocks to their work people.

G.W.E. When you were working on a string wheel you had a woman to turn the big wheel, and a second woman who, in the photograph, seems to be making the balls of clay for you to throw with.

G.M.   Yes they either called them ballers or takers off and the looker to the ware fetched your clay and carried the thrown wares on boards, turned them over and got them ready for the turner.

G.W.E. I gather that after Lockett's you went to Dudson's?

G.M.   When Lockett's closed down I thought my world had come to an end because I had concentrated on their ware. It was different to general earthenware throwing all these big thick mortars, and straight up jars and barrel jugs. I thought my world had come to an end. I finished on the Saturday at Lockett's and on the Monday morning I happened to go to Dudson's and got a job at the first minute I asked. I started work at Dudson's and I did a year there before I went to Wedgwood's.

G.W.E. What did you make at Dudson's?

G.M.   Oh jasper, general wares, everything.

G.W.E. So very different to what you had worked on at Lockett's?

G.M.   Oh totally different. In the evening of my lifetime it made it very hard for me because I'd concentrated on the work at Lockett's, and then I had to come back to general earthenware which was not so hard, not so heavy, but all the shapes I'd got to learn were new to me and I was getting on for sixty you see. That's what made it hard. All my jobs, I've held every one and never had the sack, but the work at Dudson's was at first difficult for me.

G.W.E. About this period didn't Wedgwood come into the story?

G.M.   Oh well I went to the Etruria factory. When I was at Lockett's they came to me and promised me the moon. That was in 1922, August 1922. I offered to go for them just for six months. I had a guarantee for six months. It was so much per week for six months you see. Well, when Christmas came they had two or three days play. The following week, when my wages came out, I was a couple of days' wages short. Well, I went to the manager who said, "You can't get that," he said. "I don't get it. Even if it's on order from Major Frank" he said, "you won't get it. I don't get it, Mr Tittensor doesn't get it."

   I said to him, "I don't care whether Mr Tittensor or you get it, I want mine." I went to the general manager who was Bernard Moore in those days and told him about it. He said, "Certainly; it'll come out next week." He was disgusted, the clay manager was, he didn't send me two days out the next week, he sent me one day one week and one day the following week. Of course that was the end of my career at Wedgwood's. I gave my notice in.

G.W.E. You have said that you worked on several factories all within the same week. Was it in 1929?

G.M.   I worked on five firms a week. There was supposed to be no work. I worked at Lockett's for a day, George Jones's Crescent Potteries for a day making egg cups. I went to William Adams of Tunstall making jasper, and Cauldon Place making honey pots. On a Saturday morning I used to go and do half a day at Wilshaw and Robinson's making tobacco jars. I think it might be a record!

G.W.E. You mentioned Moorcroft in an earlier conversation.
G.M.   I went there after Lockett's finally closed down. I rather liked their ware. As a matter of fact I liked Moorcroft's ware the best of all.

G.W.E. I suspect you rediscovered in Moorcroft something of the family atmosphere you experienced at Lockett's.
G.M.   Yes I did. It was another little old fashioned firm where you always had contact with your boss, you could always speak to Mr Moorcroft. Moorcroft's was a nice little firm but another job came up while I was there. I was only doing two days at Moorcroft's. The other job was with the Portmerion factory in Stoke, and it was making pestles and mortars, and full-time. Well that was right up my street. So I left Moorcroft to go to Portmerion.
    Earlier you asked me about conditions. Well, pre-war when I was a boy things were bad, and nearly everyone liked beer. One old feller used to take his waistcoat off every Monday morning, and it was my job to take it to the pawnshop. He got six pence on his waistcoat and he'd go straight off the firm across The Talbot. It would be three or four days before he came back. He had this "latch lifter" as he called it, a six pence latch lifter.
    Once he was in the pub he was alright for two or three days. It was a hell of a struggle for him to get it back at the weekend, this sixpence, so that he could pay it back.

G.W.E. Other people have said that they felt better when lubricated with a glass of beer. Some even claimed that it helped them cope with the dust.
G.M.   Oh well, I've always liked beer. As a matter of fact I don't think I would still be here if I hadn't had plenty of beer. I think there's something in beer that you can't buy out of a chemist's shop. No matter what kind of food you have, if you have hipbone steak, it might cost five shillings but if you have a pint of beer with it it's worth ten shillings.

G.W.E. What do you think about the idea that it helped to protect you from the effects of dust?
G.M.   They often say that they drank to swill the dust away. That's a fallacy because you've got to breath silicosis, it's got to go up your nostrils or down your throat. You've got to breath it. You could eat a bucketful of pure silica but it wouldn't give you silicosis. It's what you breathe, and it gets into your lungs and goes solid like cement. It stops your lungs from contracting and expanding. People with silicosis are alright if they are stationary but the moment we'll say they go up stairs or do any work their lungs won't contract and expand. They can't get their breath. You've got to breathe silica. There was one old man who worked with me who used to say they are all dying of silicosis, every few months one of your pals died, he'd got silicosis and snuffed it. He used to say to me, 'Do you know why I don't snuff it?" and do you know what his answer was? "You see those hairs up me nose. If you hadn't got those hairs up your nose the silica would go straight up. Those hairs are moist and the silica clings to them," he said. "That's what saved me."

And I think there's a lot in what he said. The dust that used to cling on those hairs up his nostrils would have gone into his lungs it it hadn't stopped there.

G.W.E. Did you know anyone who continued working despite being badly affected by dust?

G.M.   I don't think they stopped anyone. They kept giving them a certain degree of dust. In recent years the vans came round or you went to the hospital. They certified you with a certain degree of silicosis, and gave you a little pension, we'll say ten bob at first and fifteen bob for the next stage and a pound for the next stage. But I don't think they stopped anyone. They advised yer to stop but a chap with two or three kids couldn't afford to stop work you see. Oh they could come until they could hardly crawl. It was painful to look at them, and there's no cure for silicosis you know.

G.W.E. Did you ever see anyone eat their food at the bench?

G.M.   Yes I did. You know a lot of silicosis is self inflicted. Dirty workmen covering work with bags, wetting it 'til they made the shop look like a flour mill, especially when they uncovered their work. Then they were breathing it. We had cellars that they could take their work down, and keep it in proper condition. It was really idleness. They did it for their own convenience to get wages quicker. They stacked it up in the shops and covered it up. A lot of silicosis was self inflicted.

G.W.E. In the photographs taken at Lockett's they often show a large stove pot that heated the workshop. You have told me that food was sometimes heated up on them.

G.M.   It was just like going home. I used to go in a morning and at Lockett's they had a big stove pot. I would take a quarter pound of bacon and a couple of eggs. As soon as I got there I would put it on the pot. The fire had just lighted and it was half an hour before it started to sizzle but it was beautifully cooked. I've never had bacon cooked like it in me life. Oh we used to fry bloaters and cook lobby on the stove.

G.W.E. I suppose when you think about all the pots you have made it must be a great source of satisfaction to know that many of them will survive way into the future. Even when broken and discarded the fragments are virtually indestructable.

G.M.   I've always had a pride in my job, and it's that satisfaction that makes you keep throwing, why you never want to change. Another thing there are a lot of alleged connoisseurs of pottery that can't tell a cast or jollied article from something that has been thrown, whereas the thrower needs only to put his fingers inside an article and he can tell you the way it's been made. In my own little tinpot way, only on making, I always look inside being a thrower, to see if it's a good article because if it's made poorly, it's a poor article no matter what's done to it afterwards. If it's made wrong it's wrong right through.

Notes

1.   The traditional perception of the Pottery Workers' Union is that it has lacked the power and influence that was once associated with other unions eg Miners' Union and the union that represented employees in Britain's car industry of the sixties and seventies. Whilst this was an understandable overall view as far as the Potters' Union was concerned, the more unusual branches of the industry

were certainly weakly represented. In Mr Myatt's case, as a thrower, he was part of a very exclusive group even by the early decades of the last century. He and other throwers were accordingly disadvantaged in their bargaining positions, especially with the rapid steps then being made in connection with automation.

2.   Prior to the wider applications of steam power many items of equipment in the ceramic industry were dependent on human sources of power. True mechanisation was late in coming to ceramic production. In the case of John Lockett's factory they were still using a wheel that would have been turned by a male or female assistant well into the 1920s. In its essentials this type of wheel would appear identical in its construction to the wheel believed to have been used by Josiah Wedgwood to throw six commemorative vases on the opening of Etruria in 1769. A later wheel based on this pattern may be seen in the Ceramic Gallery of the Potteries Museum.

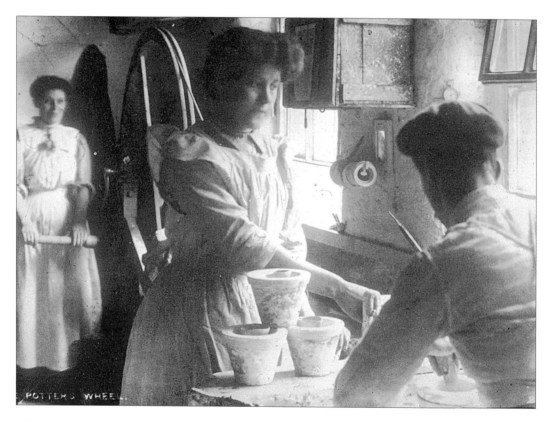

The thrower assisted by his wheel-turner and taker-off. Women and children who carried out these roles were often employed by the thrower and not the factory owner.

Jar, Lockett Factory, early 20th century. Thrown by George Myatt and supplied to pharmacies for containing leeches.

Printed lids for pots, made in this instance to contain cold cream and described by Mr Myatt as 'boxes'. These examples are not from Lockett's and date from the 1850s. Similar wares were made at the Lockett Factory.

The printing shop at Lockett's, 1932, where pot lids and similar products
received their labels etc. printed underglaze.

Hand pressing of bed pans and other medical ware, Lockett Factory, 1932.

George Myatt especially enjoyed the years he spent with Moorcroft.
He would have been responsible for throwing wares like these on this
page and opposite.

Turners and their women assistants, Lockett's, Longton, 1932. This photograph provides
interesting documentary evidence of manual labour applied to a process that was
surprisingly late in utilising mechanical power. Mrs Alice Morris began her
working life in the ceramic industry as a lathe treader.

That lathe treading was a long-established practice in the ceramic industry is borne out by
this engraving from *The Cabinet Encyclopaedia*, 1852.

Alice Morris
Lathe treader, Tower and Scolloper

Interviewed Weston Coyney, Stoke on Trent, 1974.

It was mentioned in my introduction that few women contacted me to offer their testimonies, a situation for which I have no ready explanation apart from a general reticence and modesty. Those women who did provide an interesting contrast in experiences. For example, Alice Foxall's account (to follow) reveals a degree of resentment for being forced to become a pottery worker when her ambitions were clearly directed towards a career in teaching. This experience contrasts sharply with that recounted to me by Alice Morris who entered the industry around the same time as her namesake. Despite being seventy-five at the time of our conversation she was still working as a scolloper. The enthusiasm she reveals in the account of her earliest years in the industry was still in evidence some sixty years later. In short she must have been, from her employer's standpoint, an ideal employee.

Mrs Morris provides a vivid description of the poverty that characterised the life styles of many working potters during the early decades of the last century. She recalls having to borrow her mother's shoes upon obtaining a job, the reward being that she would be allowed to spend a proportion of her first week's wages on a pair of second hand shoes.

Her account also identifies some interesting practices in the industry. In common with others I interviewed she received her wages not from the factory owner but from the man she worked for. Other, albeit unofficially acknowledged features of the industry, include the widely shared belief, especially amongst those working in the largely china-producing towns of Fenton and Longton, that there was something inherently superior about making bone china as opposed to earthenware, a belief that is difficult to justify in rational terms. The only basis for it resides in the fact that it was generally the case that bone china products were often, though not invariably, decorated in onglaze enamels and gilding. The traditional method of applying gold decoration involved using a grade of the metal that was of a high quality and that also necessitated a finishing process known as burnishing with a tool made from a hardstone such as bloodstone or agate. The late 1860s witnessed the introduction of a method of gilding that dispensed with the need for this labour-intensive procedure. This cheaper alternative to 'best gold' enabled manufacturers to make a greater use of gold decoration on earthenwares. But it is also the case that hand-painted designs were still being applied to china at a period when the cheaper decorating method that came in with the introduction of lithography was readily available.

Perhaps of greater significance is the evidence Mrs Morris provided concerning her early work as a lathe treader. Other industries at the same period had, where possible, replaced labour with mechanical methods, notably steam power, long before Mrs Morris's introduction to the pottery industry.

It would become self evident to anyone watching a lathe treader at work that the job demanded more stamina than skill. It would also, for most people, have proved monotonous and lacking in variety. This was in contrast to the turner's experience which consisted of a combination of skill and judgement. For Mrs Morris however lathe treading was, via her imagination and fortitude, transformed into an activity that was not totally devoid of any pleasurable aspects. In her interview she compares the rhythm of lathe treading to the sensation to be derived from ballroom dancing.

It is almost certain that most 19th century critics of industry would have received such a testimony with incredulity. Was she perhaps simply grateful for the opportunity to earn a living at a period when to do otherwise was a certain route to poverty? Whatever interpretation is placed on Mrs Morris's description of her experience it clearly reveals a personality distinguished by honesty and vitality.

Lathe treader and turner.

Alice Morris

I started to work when I was thirteen. The first thing I had to do was that I had to borrow my mother's shoes to go to work in. We lived in Wellington Court at the bottom of New Street in Longton. I got a job at the nearest potbank to where I lived. That was at New Street in Longton. When I went for a job the manager said, "Go up and see Mr Sherratt because you don't look as if you'll be strong enough for the job. " I thought to myself he's mistaken. I didn't know how strong I was but I felt determined. So of course I said, "Well if I get the job how much will it be?" He said, "Well it'll be sixpence a day, that's three shillings a week, but don't forget", he said, "You'll only work till one o'clock on Saturdays." I said, "Right, that will do for me." Three shillings seemed a lot of money then. Anyway I went up and he said, "Do you think you could do a heavy job?" I said, "Yes I can, would you like to show me what it is?" He said, "Well it won't take much showing. See that wheel on the bench?" I said, "Yes". He said, "That handle, if you can turn it round and keep turning it all day until you have your breaks, then I can make my plates." That wheel, with the handle, you turned it and it drove pulleys so that his jigger could go round to make the plates. That's what they call a jigger.

He said, "But if you care to you can have an extra sixpence a week if you want to do that all the time, providing it suits me, and if you're strong enough because it's got to go at a certain speed." He said, "I've got another girl here, she does the mould running." I turned the wheel so that he could make the plates, and it had to go at a certain speed.

Of course it's all done different today. He said, "Of course before I come to work you'll have to clean the fireplace out and get the coal in. Other than that you can wedge the clay. Which would you like to do?" I thought to myself wedging the clay seems more important, I'll let that other girl do the job of taking the ashes down and carrying coal up, and starting off the fire. He said, "Incidentally, you'll have to bring your own sticks." So I thought if she's going to do that job I'll see she gets sticks, because we go across the banks picking them. Anyway he said, "I'll give you a day on it. It's rather stiff on the arms." I couldn't sleep all that night, and couldn't get there quick enough. I thought before I went to bed I haven't got any shoes decent enough to go in. Me Mam said, "You can go in mine for this week, and then we can go down to Fanny Dean's and get a pair secondhand." We could get them for three ha'pence then you know. Fanny Dean lived just above the bank (potbank), top of the street. I couldn't wait all that first week to think I was going to Fanny Dean's to get a pair of secondhand shoes of my own. Anyway I went to work the next morning.

I was ready for anything. I didn't feel hunger although we never had enough to eat, we were right down on food. I didn't feel hungry because I was too anxious. Anyway when I got there it was fascinating to me you know. He kept saying, "Don't go too quick. You'll learn in time the speed I need." But trouble of it was it went so slow, I'm a person who likes to be on their feet running about you know. I thought to myself I have picked the wrong job. That girl's going to run in and out of the stove with those moulds and I'm going to be standing here. Then I thought still never mind it's an extra sixpence a week, I'll stick to it for that extra sixpence. Anyway when I went the next day he said, "What are your arms like?" I said, "It isn't me arms as much as me wrist, and me shoulder." "Oh you'll get used to that," he said, "When you've done a day or two at it."

The first week that I did I thought to myself it's interesting to think all them plates in there have been put in through me. That's how I thought you know. The next morning he said, "Now don't forget I wouldn't let you do it the first day but you'll have to go down to the slip house and carry some clay up on your shoulder, and then I'll show you what to do with it." He got a long piece of wire with a stick on either end like they used to use to cut cheese. He said, "You get this big lump of clay." I said, "Shall I fetch two lots up then so that I can wedge them together?" "Just please yourself" he said. "When I come to work I want some good clay." Believe me in them days it was clay. It was just the same as cutting butter. Anyway I brought it up and put it on the bench. You had to get this wire, and cut the clay through. You then picked up the top piece, held it high above your head, and then banged it down. Then you turned it over and did the same thing until it was all smooth.

This man I worked for had some dirty habits. He used to spit a lot. I was very poor but I was clean and I didn't like what he did but I never complained. He used to say, "You've done a good job there kid, that's the best bit of wedging I've seen." But I didn't like the man, he was very dirty and scruffy.

The next morning I got more clay for him. The first thing I saw him do was to look on the bench and go "mmm" as much as to say, "She's doing well". One day he said, "You don't talk much do you?" I turned round and said, "Well, I haven't got much time really have I? If I do much talking I shall go down on my speed." I've got an idea he wanted to make a bit of fuss of me because he thought he'd dropped on a good, you know, sensible girl. The other girl used to look across at me as much as to say, "He never talks to me." Later I got used to him and I'd help the other girl take her ashes out, you know, and because I'd only got to come from the bottom street see, and this other girl had to come from Fenton, me and her got on really good terms.

I couldn't wait for Saturday. They (the workmen) paid us out you know, not the bosses, the men paid us out. So he said, "Here you are duck, there s 3/6d there, you've done very well, and I'm very pleased with you." He said, "My wages have gone up four bob." I thought "Good Lord!" Anyway, he said, "I'll be seeing you on Monday. Oh, by the way", he said, "You've got to clear up you know." I was about to cart off. I had to clean all his dirt out. I thought to myself, it's passing time anyhow.

When I went off the potbank there was a little toffee shop across the road and I'd got this two shilling piece and a shilling and sixpenny piece. I'd never handled money like that before. I don't think I'd ever even seen it because your parents never let you see anything. Anyway I went across the shop and said "Please could you change me a two shilling piece?" The man said, "Yes. How would you like it?" I said, "Could you give it me in pennies?" "Do you want 24?" he said. I said, "Yes" Then I said, "Now can you change me a shilling?" He said, "Well, no I haven't got enough." So I thought to myself never mind. I just wanted this big handful of money.

I got home to my mother; I thought she'd say "good" but she just took it and didn't say anything. So I said, "By the way what about going to Fanny Dean's, Mam, for some shoes for next week?" She said, "Yes you can, here's sixpence to get a pair." I got a pair of shoes and off I went to work.

Now, each week I got used to this man, and his way of working - you know you're supposed to put your hand in a bowl of water to smooth your clay, but he used to spit on it.

One day I asked him why he did it. You see he used to chew baccer all day, and of course it was making saliva all the time in his mouth. The other girl couldn't care less. One day I said to him, "Do you have to spit on your clay?" He said, "It saves time wench. I don't have to keep dipping me hands in water all day." Sometimes he would say to me, "Would you fetch us a pint from the Three Tuns?" And this was in my breakfast time. I used to go across - pubs were open all day from six in a morning. Sometimes he'd say, "I've had a little tot of rum before coming in." Well, it was only three ha'pence for a tot then. He never had any breakfast, just his dinner.

When I'd been with him for six or seven months I thought to myself I wish I could get something a bit better. If it's the same money I'd manage, but I daren't mention it to my mother. She used to say, "Whatever are you polishing them shoes for?' I said, "Because there's white on them." She said, "When you came home last night you said you liked white on your shoes to let people see you had been to work."

Well, the girl I worked with finished, so he says to me, "I don't know what I'm going to do. I'll get you - instead of putting the fire in - to set all the moulds, put ''em on the bench for me to make the plates,and then you can run them in." In other words he was having me do two jobs. He said, "It won't last for long and anyway I'll give you extra wages for it." It lasted for about three or four days and then he got another girl to do the job.

I stuck it for about six months and I heard one of the girls say, "They want a lathe treader round the corner," I said, "Where?" She said, "Round Pool's." I said what's lathe treading, because I'd never been in another clay shop? She said, "Oh it's hard work, but you'll get more money." Well, I thought to myself this is it. At dinner time I went round and saw a Mr Colclough - that's him as opened a potbank afterwards, but he was a manager then. I said, "Mr Colclough, do you want a learner lathe treader?" He said, "I want somebody who has already learned the job." I said, "Well I've never done it but if you'll give me a chance I'm willing to learn." He said, "I'll tell you what I'll do. I'll take this young lad we're training, and you can both train together. I think you'll do better that way." So I said, "How much is the money?" He said, "It's 3/6d." It was the same. But don't forget I'd be learning a trade. Cup handling and them things, you know, you had to learn.

I went to work with this boy, and I liked it. Now, this job was with a big wheel. Attached to this wheel there was a plank that I had to put my foot on and press it down all day to take the wheel that spun the part round that the turner put the cup on. I loved it because I wanted to be on my feet all the time. It reminded me of when I was dancing.

I worked alongside the boy who was learning for about twelve months, and I didn't get any extra wages, just the 3/6d, but I felt I was doing something special. At first I didn't say anything to my mother. Anyway when I came home one day she said, "Anybody would think you'd been to church, you've got no white on your shoes." I said, "Well, I'll tell you why - I've gone and got myself another job." "Why didn't you tell me?" mother said. My answer was, "Because you might have said no, and I want to better myself." She said, "You should have asked my permission to leave one job to go to another." I said, "Well I'll tell you straight, I didn't like the man I was working for."

That was enough for mother, and that was my trade until I was fifty-four - from fourteen to fifty-four. When the 1914/18 War broke out I stuck with it. When the War was on they were running everywhere after lathe treaders because married women, whose husbands were at the War, wouldn't go to work. Then they weren't the same as they are today. Women today will strive for money. I think myself they didn't think then there was much prospect if they did. What they want now is fancy numbers. Then they didn't. As long as there was food on the table that was enough.

One day somebody said to me, "Alice they've been running round after lathe treaders. There's a man been your house." My father was at the War. I took this job on and it was Hanson's, Sandford Hill. Now, when I went they said, "This is on the head lather, can you do it?" I said yes. Mind you, to be honest, I couldn't really because I was only a trainee so far. So the boss said, "It's going to be a heavy job you know." I said, "In which way?" He said, "Well it's on egg cups and you have to go at a hell of a speed" - and you do. He said, "For bowls and sugars you go slower but it's much heavier." I said, "Well, I can do it, what are the wages?" I always wanted to know how much it was you know. He said, "You'll be piece work and you should knock a quid out." I thought to myself a quid, and that was it.

It was while I got this job that mother was taken ill, and I had to run dinner from the top of Sandford Hill to the Catholic Church in Longton. It was a good way you know. She was ill in bed for a week but I didn't realise she was so ill. They took her into hospital and she died. I was left to look after four younger children. My father was at the front in France because with him being on reserve he had to go straight away as soon as the War broke out. I had that job, and I looked after the children all the way through the War. And how old would I be, I'd only be about eighteen when the War finished. Then I got another job.

They said I'd get more money at this job so I said who is it for? They said with Dick Bennett. I said I don't know him, where does he work? They said he works at Minton's down Stoke. "Stoke" I said, "Oh I can't go if it isn't going to pay my tram fare." It seemed as if they wanted a good lathe treader, because the women that were married wouldn't go. So anyway I went and saw him at his house and he said, "Well, you should get about thirty bob a week." I said, "That's it then I'll give my notice in," which I did and went down to Minton, in Stoke.

I stuck it with him till I was twenty and then got married in a hurry. A chap, a neighbour's boy, and my father had come home from the forces. Things were going right, the kids we're growing up but my father used to drink because he got pretty fair money. This boy, who was going out to India, came home for a few days and said, "Alice should we get married?" I said, "Well, I might as well" because life then didn't have anything better to offer me. We got married in three days by special licence. He had said, "I want to get married on the condition that you will come to India." I said, "Great, that'll be good for me." Anyway we married.

In the meantime I got another job at Radford's in Fenton. I thought to myself it's nearer to and it's only while waiting to go to India. It was absolutely lovely working there. There was no heavy machinery, no noise. The only noise was me. I was singing all day. I always used to be singing because I'd got a pretty good voice you know, and I loved it. But today you can't hear anybody singing, the noise of the machinery is horrible.

G.W.E. So you had made a good move. What did you think of your new employers?

A.M. Lovely people they were. It was better than having your own father when you hadn't got a good father of your own. You used to sort of lean on them you know. If anybody hadn't got any wages in the first week you could go and they'd lend you a bit. Well, you couldn't do that today, no. I like going to work but it hasn't got the interest it used to have, by any means. The young people today, their work is rubbish. My scolloping is done twenty times slower but it's really good work, not like theirs. I don't know how the firm can sell most of it, no I don't.

I had an express letter from India, and it said, "Don't bother coming." All the preparations were made, and everything. It said, "Your husband is coming home, he's got cancer of the lung." Him having to come home, that was the beginning of the end, of deep poverty once again. I had only just managed to get on my feet, drawing wages and looking after them. So of course when he came home I went to work as usual down at Colclough's on the lathe. But people in them days were absolutely marvellous. You could just walk in and say, "Well, I haven't got anything for breakfast, I just want a piece of bread and butter." Somebody would say, "Oh well here you are, here's a penny, go and get some for your breakfast." Something like that. That wouldn't happen today. It was like one big family.

When I was at work I had two children in between. It was all poverty you know, and what little bit I was at home was on the Parish Relief which didn't suit me. When I buried Jim I went to work for T.C. Wildes and I enjoyed it. Mr Kenneth, he'd walk through in a morning and say, "Good morning girls" and some of the boys would say, "He never says good morning to us." I said, "Well, you're not as good looking as us you know."

If you had anything wrong with your work you'd carry your boards out. You had to carry all your own work out on boards which they'd put on two stands right in the middle of the bank. There was no concealing anything. They'd go right along the board to see if anything was wrong, and if there was they'd kick the board up, and that was your loss. I still think that's why they kept their trade. They kept the tradition because your work had to be perfect in them days.

Then they brought out these casting machines. Ware was previously made solid by a thrower. A thrower had a woman to get the clay, cut it and then to knock it up and make it into a ball. You would give it to him and he made a lining first. Then when they'd filled the bench with these linings he made them into cups. Well, today everything's done by casting. There's nothing solid done unless it's on the big dinnerware made in Burslem - I suppose there they are still made by hand with solid clay. There may not be any made this way today. I don't really know because I've never worked in earthenware.

G.W.E. So most of your work then was in the southern end of the city, and you handled almost exclusively bone china?

A.M. Yes. Longton is all china isn't it? Fenton is the same. But when you go to Stoke, Hanley, Burslem, Tunstall it's earthenware, nearly all earthenware. I've never worked in earthenware. They always used to say that them who worked in earthenware were on the rough side. I'm not being negative but they seemed a little bit on the rough side. They'd wear anything you know, whereas in china I think we were a little bit more sophisticated. We used to have to buy our own sponges when I was a girl and our own oil for the lathe.

G.W.E. So the turner didn't buy these things?
A.M.   No he didn't. Work on the potbank was more peaceful in them days, it was a pleasure. They used to settle (pay out) on Thursdays and often you could tell who'd had a good week and who hadn't. Workers who had got a good week would be singing. Today you wouldn't hear anybody singing because of the machinery.

G.W.E. During your years in the industry you must have witnessed many changes.
A.M.   Oh yes, and don't ask me if it's been for the best. I'd say no, no. The homeliness of life on the banks has gone. Today the girls who start work at fifteen class themselves with my age. They talk to you as though you are a child. Now, when I was young you didn't speak until you were spoken to. Another thing, you wouldn't have dared to go to work with make-up on or anything like that. Well you couldn't afford make-up but if you could you wouldn't be classed as a good girl. But I don't think like that because I'm an old person - I definitely live young, and I dress young, as young as any of them. But girls today are not the same. There's too much money about today, and people haven't got the time for the other person in the same shop. I've got some people where I work now who are in their fifties and have been in the industry since they were thirteen. Now we can talk together about the old times. But not with the younger ones, they don't want to know. We were dedicated. I'm very precise about how I do my scolloping.

G.W.E. For the benefit of those of us who are unfamiliar with the term can you explain what scolloping is?
A.M.   When you get the cup from the mould, when it's not in a very dry state, you have a knife and you have to cut round the tops of cups and sugars to make a pattern, a little pattern on it. Then you rub it down with your fingers to make it a half round surface on the top. You then go over it with a sponge. But scolloping wasn't really my trade, it was the trade I had to pick up when I was fifty odd.

G.W.E. So scolloping followed lathe treading?
A.M.   Lathe treading went out when casting came in. Turners had to train for other jobs.

G.W.E. At the age of seventy-five you are still working in the industry. This must be a rare distinction. Were there any other members of your family working in the industry?
A.M.   My two sisters, and they were also lathe treaders. But they finished work when they were about fifty.

G.W.E. Were your parents potters?
A.M.   My mother never went to work, and my father had probably never been on a potbank. He was supposed to be a collier but he didn't go all that often.

G.W.E. So you were the first member of your immediate family to go into potting?

A.M.   Yes I was.

G.W.E. In what leisure time you had, after a day's work, say at the age of fifteen onwards, what did you do. I take it there wasn't much to do except to rest for the next day?
A.M.   If there was anything to be done mother would make sure I did it. If I had half a day off she would say, "Well, you can go and scrub upstairs". I was scrubbing two rooms because there wasn't any carpets. When I was scrubbing the stairs she'd say, "Don't knock on the sides - I want to hear the bristles not the wood." I'm much the same myself, I'm pretty strict with the children.

   Potting is a lovely industry for being together. I feel it a bit now because two or three of my friends have died. You just can't go back to where you'd like to.

Longton, early 20th century.

In my interview with Leonard Potts he describes the skills required for
china plate making on a jigger. The fixed profile shown here was better
suited to earthenware compositions.

Leonard Potts
Hand plate maker

Interviewed Hanley, Stoke on Trent, 1976.

How long does it take for something to be regarded as a traditional practice in manufacturing, twenty, fifty or a hundred years? Clearly the answer depends on the age of the industry in question. In the case of ceramic production the making of pots by coiling, or some alternative non-mechanical methods, may be traced back, via archaeological evidence, to a period long before the advent of written records. The semi-mechanical process of throwing clay on a wheel or turntable was practised in certain parts of the world in pre-biblical times. The forming of clay in moulds was also known in Egypt and China at an early period, certainly before the Bronze Age.

At a much later period, for example the Song dynasty (906-1279AD) in China, it occurred to someone that circular forms could be made over a mould attached to a potter's wheel, the upper or face side of the dish or plate being formed by the mould while the underside was shaped with a profile. Although not calling upon the same order of skill as throwing moulding, nevertheless, demanded from its practitioners a period of training. By the 18th century forms, originally designed for production in a metal, such as silver, copper and even gold, were widely copied by manufacturers of porcelain, earthenware and stoneware. Hollow forms such as jugs, teapots and vases were thrown, hand pressed in plaster-of-Paris moulds and more rarely at this relatively early date, slipcast. Flat shapes such as plates were being increasingly made by the middle years of the 18th century according to a principle very similar to that devised by the Song dynasty Chinese potter, in other words with a profile and mould.

A dictionary definition of 'traditional' says that it is something handed down orally or by example. In the case of plate-making with a mould and profile the tradition varied slightly within different factories and industrial societies. The one feature that appears to have been fairly constant was that it was a skill performed by men. This was certainly the case in North Staffordshire. The main reason for the apparent male prerogative was that its exponents could demand a higher than average wage for their labours. It was generally the case that in the 19th century Staffordshire industry hand flatware makers or pressers were amongst the better paid members of any workforce.

For employers of the day this was something of a problem because it automatically conferred on flatware makers a strong bargaining position. The status in making wares this way lay in the judgement and manipulative skill associated with holding the profile, a tool usually made from clay and subsequently fired. Too much pressure on the profile would lead to an unacceptably thin object while an inadequate degree of pressure produced the opposite, namely a plate that was too thick. Spinning the mould on its turntable was done with one hand while holding the profile with the other.

It was almost inevitable that someone would attempt to improve on this essentially ancient technique. In 1840 an engineer/inventor named George Wall took out a patent, along with a pottery manufacturer named John Ridgway, for: "Certain improvements in the mode of preparing bats of earthenware and porcelain clay, and of forming or shaping them into articles of earthenware and porcelain, and in the machinery or apparatus applicable thereto. Instead of hand labour, passing a lump of clay through a pair of common squeezing rollers or cylinders, and so forming a bat. Shaping or forming articles of earthenware or porcelain clays by means of a profile used in combination with a revolving mould, or vice versa, and also in combination with self-acting feeding and delivering apparatus or driven by steam or other power."

Arguably the most important feature of the Wall-Ridgway patent, that incidentally the specification fails to make clear, concerns the proposal to attach the profile to a handle that the operative would bring down onto the rotating clay. In other words the need for judgement and skill was removed because the thickness of an article being made could be predetermined by the adjustment of a screw. Mention of steam power also identifies the other important feature of the patent namely that instead of being dependent on manpower the driving mechanism was provided by an engine.

Once it became known that Ridgway and other manufacturers had installed the new-fangled machine there was immediate alarm amongst the district's male jigger operators. They feared that it would immediately lead to a downgrading of their occupation, and what was probably considered even worse, the work would be handed over to women. The resulting opposition to Wall's patent led to industrial action and a search for some suitably effective resistance to their employers' enthusiasm for what they perceived to be an important and highly desirable innovation. The full story of this movement is long and detailed. In short a local trades union leader named William Evans believed that a solution lay in an emigration scheme to the North American state of Wisconsin. He argued that by creating a labour shortage in the Potteries towns those workers who chose not to take part in the scheme, and therefore remained in the Potteries, would take on a higher value in the labour market. Although several families actually followed the idea through by emigrating to America during the late 1840s the scheme eventually failed. From the outset it was an idea born of desperation.

In due course mechanised plate-making, along with other schemes to revolutionise ceramic production, was accepted by the industry in general. My interview with Leonard Potts was interesting for a variety of reasons, not least the evidence it provided concerning the continuing practice of hand plate-making in the bone china sector of the industry. However, Mr Potts' skills by the late 1940s were almost as rare as those of George Myatt interviewed earlier. It is particularly significant that his plate-making by hand was practised at the Spode factory, a leading maker of bone china. In common with other contributors Leonard Potts was especially conscious of the deleterious effects of dust being, himself a victim of silicosis.

Leonard Potts

I'm now retired after working in clay for fifty-one years. I left school at fourteen and started to work at Josiah Wedgwood at Etruria as a mould runner. To the uninitiated this was a factotum to china-plate makers, the wages were 7/6d for forty-eight hours. On my first day at work I was set upon by youths and girls, all laughing. They daubed my genitals with oil and clay slurry. This was a ritual then. If it happened today they would be sent up for an indecent assault.

When I was fifteen I became an apprentice china plate-maker. In those days bone china was made by hand. You had your clay and took a lump, put it onto a plaster-of-Paris bed and knocked it into shape with a hand batter. The hand batter was made of fired saggar marl with a handle. The bottom half was also plaster-of-Paris. You made your bat of clay to resemble a round piece of pastry. I then picked up this round piece of clay with my left hand while putting my right hand at the back and threw it on to a plaster mould. I then set the mould, which was attached to a turntable, in motion. While the wheel was in motion I shaped it by applying a hand tool and smoothed it with pitchers. This is where the craft came in because you had no set gauge, the gauge was in your sense of feel. If you made your plate too thick, or too thin, it was no good, and you did not get any pay for it.

The working day was eight and a half hours, and on Saturdays I worked four and a half hours. I used to walk from near Stoke football ground (Victoria Ground) to Etruria every morning, and back at night. If it was raining my mother would give me one penny to travel by tram to Howard Place (Shelton), which was a good halfway of my journey. I liked my job. Anyone watching a potter will see the changing shape of the clay until eventually he produces a plate. This was then dried, leaving a rough edge which was removed with a sharpened piece of tin, and then sponged until the surface was almost like glass. Then it is ready to have its first fire called the biscuit. The method of china-plate making has altered vastly in my fifty years in the industry. Plate-making was once a craft.

In this industry we can contract silicosis. I have it but not bad enough to warrant a disability pension. I can't walk for a good distance without stopping to admire the scenery. You get a tightness in the chest caused by fine particles of dust in the air. If you get a shaft of sunlight in the workshop it's possible to see the dust floating in the atmosphere. A great deal has been done as regards progress to minimise the danger of contracting the disease. When I was a mould-runner I wore a twill apron, which held the dust. Today we wear nylon overalls to which the dust won't adhere.

The foregoing was from a prepared script. The following was prompted by my questions.

G.W.E. Your mention of a hand profile is interesting because a tool that matches your description was used until the middle years of the 19th century in connection with the production of plates, whether in earthenware or bone china. In the 1830s certain manufacturers introduced a machine for making plates that brought down a profile onto a bat of clay laid over a mould. So it is both surprising and interesting that anyone was using a hand-held profile in the 20th century.

L.P.   In the firm where I was working (Spode) we still retained the old-fashioned methods of china plate making. A lot of this was due to a lack of capital for buying new machines, plus, at that time, we had a very good boss named Mr Gresham Copeland, who was very keen to keep everything that was old and good.

G.W.E. You have with you a profile that has a date on it of 1863. I take it this profile was on the factory when you joined Spode. Was it handed over to you by someone who taught you the job of plate making?
L.P.   We had an old warehouse that was dismantled and replaced by a new building. A lot of these old profiles were kept in this place so I had one or two of them for souvenirs. For all the current lines, especially the popular lines, each plate had a different profile. A ten inch plate profile would not make a ten inch scalloped plate.

G.W.E. The remarkable thing is although it is made of fired and glazed earthenware it's still in good condition. It was obviously never broken despite being used daily, presumably for several years. How many plates could you make in a day using this type of profile and a whirler?
L.P.   I used to make about eight dozen ten inch plates in a day with a hand profile. Today, working on a hand jolley, making the same plates, and all the same conditions, I could make fifty dozen a day. With plate-making today at my old firm, you put a ball of clay onto a whirling plaster-of-Paris block, a blade comes down at the same time, spreading out the clay to whatever thickness is required. This you pick off the block and then, as we did fifty years ago, throw it on a mould. While the mould is whirling an arm is brought down on which a tool is fixed. This is almost like pulling a beer pump handle, and the plate is made.

     Another method for plain, simple shapes is called semi-automatic. As in the previous operation you put a ball of clay onto a plaster block. The blade comes down, spreads the clay, and again you throw this onto the mould. The arm comes down automatically to shape the plate. This operative will make a 120 dozen plates a day. The handmade plate was perfection, a semi-automatic made one is not in the same class, but the manufacturers had to produce more to make it profitable. On the hand plate-making if you sent a hundred plates in, you could guarantee ninety-eight coming off the kiln in biscuit. Sometimes you might get a bit of dirt on a plate. Now, with the hand jolley, I'm not talking now about the hand profile, a chap could send a hundred plates in and probably get seventy-five out.

G.W.E. So, really, with the introduction of mechanisation to plate making, despite what you have just said, given its capacity for a greatly increased output, the quantities of good wares from the kiln was actually increased?
L.P.   Yes, definitely. Today everything is done on trains and lines, intermittent kilns have now practically vanished. The bottle kiln where the saggar used to be carried on the placer's head, each plate was placed in an individual saggar. Today, each plate, as regards china, is put in a setter. Where we used to get a bung, we'll say ten high, of hand-made plates, the same height now in setters would take twenty, creating a big saving in space.

G.W.E. When you first started in the industry you said you were a mould runner?
L.P.   Yes, as a little labourer for the plate maker. If they thought you had an aptitude for

the job then you were put on a bench, but in those days you were lucky to get a bench because there were such a lot of boys waiting for jobs. If you minded your p's and q's, and you could stand one or two kicks up the backside, you were alright.

G.W.E. When you say it was a difficult job was it difficult in the sense that you were expected to work extra hard as a mouldrunner?

L.P. As a mouldrunner I ran with the moulds to a drier. At Wedgwood in those days the method of drying involved a continual fire underneath the floor of the workshop. These drying cabinets were placed on top of the drying floors. As you walked over this hot floor every day your feet used to get like pieces of liver.

G.W.E. From what people have told me it's obvious that many factories, at least at the beginning of this century, retained techniques and processes that perhaps would have been more at home in the 19th century. When you first went to work, was it at Wedgwood?

L.P. Yes, I was there until I was about twenty-two at the time of the Depression. Things were very bad. I've seen men fainting in the dole queue waiting to get their money. They really were terrible days. But we never had any bother in the potting industry. I'm really proud to have been a a part of it.

G.W.E. Was this due partly to the fact that many pottery factories were family-owned?

L.P. Oh I've touched my forelock, "Good morning Mr Spencer," that sort of thing. Oh yes.

G.W.E. Nonetheless these relationships were good, weren't they?

L.P. They knew everybody, they were great. I can't speak too highly of them. Other than dust, which was the biggest menace - we used to have a lot of stone and silica in the clays in the old days. A lot of this has been, I wouldn't say altogether, stopped. There's still a small amount in it but the stone used to cause the trouble with your chest, and we used to have lectures on dust. If you patted your clothes with your hand when you were coming off the factory at night there was a cloud of dust. Now everything is so different, all nylon overalls. I don't think there are as many deaths today from silicosis as there were in those days.

G.W.E. Were you encouraged to sweep the workshops at the end of the day, and to leave your dirty clothing behind at the factory?

L.P. Today everyone has got his own locker and, of course, you always keep your own bench clean. But speaking of fifty years ago you'd leave the clay there and we had a chap who used to come round sweeping at night, with a mask over his face. But even he died of silicosis. The life of a china potter on those days was round about forty or forty-five. They couldn't get their breath.

G.W.E. I get the impression that there were two ways of making plates depending on whether you were using a china or earthenware body. Was there a reason for this?

L.P. Oh yes. In china, during my early years, we always used the hand profile method at both factories that I worked at. Now with earthenware you can knock that about. This is where hand jolley and semi-automatic machines came in for the production of earthenware but they did not do it in china.

G.W.E. This was probably because china bodies are less plastic or shorter than earthenware.

[Plate-making.]

Skilled, and hence better paid work, was invariably a preserve of male
workers. This engraving from *The Penny Magazine* of 1848 shows a male
plate-maker working with a hand jigger. Mechanisation, introduced to this
stage of the manufacturing process during the 1840s, received a hostile
reception amongst men flatware makers.

NOTICE TO EMIGRANTS.

FITZHUGH, WALKER, AND Co., 12, GOREE PIAZZAS

LIVERPOOL,

Despatch Fine First-class American Ships,

Of large Tonnage, for the following Ports, viz :

NEW YORK,
PHILADELPHIA,
BALTIMORE,

BOSTON,
and
NEW ORLEANS,

And which are intended to sail punctually on their appointed days, They are fitted up expressly for the comfort and convenience of Cabin, Second Cabin, and Steerage Passengers. Persons about to emigrate, may save themselves the expense and delay of waiting in Liverpool, by writing a letter addressed as above, which will be immediately answered, the lowest Price of Passage told them, and they will be enabled to go direct on board the Ship, immediately on their arrival in Liverpool, thus saving the Expense of Lodging, &c. And should F. W. and Co., detain any Ship after the appointed Time, Passengers will be paid for detention.

Passengers will be found by the Ships with the full quantity of Biscuit, Flour, Oatmeal, Rice, and Potatoes, according to Act of Parliament, without extra charge.

☞ Every information will be given by applying as above, or to Mr. THOMAS COWARD, King Street, Burslem

An advertisement from *The Potters Examiner* prompted in part by William Evans's Potters' Emigration Scheme. Evans believed that by creating a labour shortage in the Potteries he would ward off the employers' plans for increased mechanisation.

Century Street, Hanley.

L.P.   We used to call it "nesh".

G.W.E. Was this when you went over to jolleying china clay?
L.P.   In the late 1940s, when I was at Spode, we did go over then to hand jolleying, as regards china, because something had to be done to increase production. We couldn't get boys to come into the trade to make china because they wouldn't have it in those days. Most of the young boys in this area were going to Michelin. So we had to devise some method for getting more plates made and so we started to develop the hand jolley for china. But if you set the hand jolley for china correct you made a good plate.

G.W.E. When you were first asked to make a plate with a machine, as opposed to using the hand-held profile, did you feel at that time this was a bad thing or did you welcome the idea?
L.P.   I did feel that it was a bad thing because I thought it was a derogatory step. I thought I was going down instead of going up.

G.W.E. You call it hand jolleying. What would you call the method using the hand-held profile?
L.P.   Hand profile.

G.W.E. Who actually made the profiles, and did you see any being made?
L.P.   You would carve a profile to suit your own individual grip. The profile was held by your forefinger and the next finger to it and held steadily while the plate was whirling. You made that profile to fit between those two fingers. If someone else had made it his grip wouldn't suit my grip.

G.W.E. Were you paid for making profiles?
L.P.   No!

G.W.E. What about the tool you used for polishing plates. Was it usual for the plate-maker to make them or did you get someone else to make them?
L.P.   You made your own pitchers. I don't know if you ever remember the old port wine bottles? They were an oval bottle. Well, we used to make a pitcher, and just put it on that oval and bend it to that shape. These again were fired biscuit, not glazed, and with their continual use they developed a polish of their own. So much so that when you'd finished your plate you could very nearly see your face in it.

G.W.E. So after you had produced the underside shape of your plate with the profile what would be the next step after that?
L.P.   It was then put into a cabinet to dry. Usually you could fetch it out of the cabinet the next morning. There was a rough edge on the rim which had to be fettled. This was smoothed off with a sharpened piece of tin and nowadays we use what we call tow. In some cases nylon tow, which is almost like cotton wool, to finish the face off and to make it nice and smooth. In my younger days we used to use sponges. Also in those days there was no dust extraction when you were doing this job. You would get your nostrils filled with it and you couldn't see. They didn't have dust extraction. Today the factory inspectors come round.

G.W.E. Was it your job to do the fettling?

L.P.   Yes, I used to do my own fettling. You produced a plate from clay right through to its first firing to biscuit.

G.W.E. So they didn't employ someone else to do this job?

L.P.   Not in my younger days, no. Today there are rows of girls doing the job we call towing and in some cases fettling.

G.W.E. When you went into the industry was it ever suggested that you might go into something else, or was it inevitable that you would become a potter?

L.P.   I've only got one regret. My biggest pal I have at Spode is a thrower. I've often wished that I could throw.

G.W.E. Were any members of your family in the industry?

L.P.   My two brothers worked at a tile firm, Minton Hollins at Stoke, and also my wife worked for the same firm, but my father was a collier.

A one dollar note issued by the Potters' Emigration Scheme for the purchase of agricultural land in the United States. The scheme ultimately failed through lack of funds and worker support.

Alice Foxall
Cup handler

Interviewed Shelton, Stoke on Trent, 1974

While it is easy to condemn the factory owners of Scriven's and Baker's day for being indifferent to the hardship of their employees, the early 20th century witnessed a dramatic change in attitudes with some factory owners demonstrating an impressive largesse in their provision of amenities for their workers from sick clubs to garden fetes held at their private homes. In many cases these gestures were reciprocated on the employee's part with an increased conscientiousness and sense of loyalty. It was more than coincidental that those people I interviewed, who expressed a particularly high level of satisfaction in connection with their work, almost without exception, spoke very highly of their employers.

It would be both biased and naive to assume that in instances of conflict and disagreement the fault was always on the employer's part. To provide just one example. In Alice Foxall's interview, to follow, she recalls that those workers responsible for firing and emptying the ovens would, almost as a matter of routine, have jugs of ale brought to them as a reward for working under the unusually hot conditions that were an inevitable feature of retrieving the hot wares after firing. However, surviving documentary evidence from the 19th century tells a story of regular disputes between employer and employee because losses had resulted from excessive drinking on the part of certain workers. The seriousness of these disputes has to be assessed in the context of such practices as 'good from oven'. In reality it meant that seriously imperfect wares from a firing might not be paid for. It is easy to see that in introducing a thoughtful gesture, such as the provision of ale, the factory owner was inadvertently paving the way for potential problems.

In an age where a policy of equal opportunities for all is the aim, if not always the reality, the possibilities for self improvement are there for anyone with the necessary self motivation and staying power. Needless to say when my contributors left school the democracy of choice was denied to a majority of the population. Mrs Alice Foxall, who I interviewed in 1974, was very honest in revealing her responses to the rules and practices imposed by her employer. She mentions her refusal to follow an established ritual which said that any wares judged to be below standard should be publicly destroyed by the worker responsible. On another occasion she mentions an incident involving some large meat dishes over which she walked to avoid going round them. Her supervisor enquired as to who was responsible. She chose not to confess. I suspect that underlying these incidents was a general resentment that factory life was forced upon her when, given the choice, she would have preferred to be a teacher.

These confessions apart her testimony confirms several interesting references to such issues as lead poisoning, and her employer's remedial measures to reduce the severity of its effects, the serious problems resulting from her fellow workers' exposure to dust, and on a lighter side an incident involving a birthday celebration and a bottle of sherry.

CAUTION

TO

PERSONS TIPPLING,

AND TO

PUBLICANS.

THE UNDERSIGNED MANUFACTURERS of Earthen-Ware within the parish of BURSLEM, sustaining the most serious loss and inconvenience, by daily interruptions to their business, in consequence of the habits of idleness and tippling which many of their workmen indulge in, during the regular hours of work, and in which they find encouragement by the very CULPABLE CONDUCT OF MANY PUBLICANS within this parish; Do hereby make known, that from the publication of this Notice, *they are resolved to give every protection and support to such persons as will lay complaints before the Magistrates, against any workmen for the offence of tippling ;* and the undersigned Manufacturers have also resolved,

Individually to notice and to report to the Magistrates

The conduct of all such Publicans as shall from henceforth suffer any workmen to remain tippling, in their houses during the regular working hours, or at any other improper time.

THE PUBLICANS ARE HEREBY INFORMED,

That on conviction of the offence of suffering tippling, or unlawful Games in their houses, they are liable to *forfeit their recognizances,* and to have their *licenses suspended* for the space of *three years,* besides being subject to a penalty of ten shillings for every offence by tippling ; and that *the Magistrates acting for this Hundred have come to the resolution of putting these laws strictly in force for the future.*

☞ Any person found tippling in a Public-house is liable to a penalty of three shillings and four-pence, to the use of the Poor, besides the costs of the information.

Burslem, November, 1815.

Wood & Caldwell	Jno. & Rich. Riley	Jno. Rogers
Henshall & Williamsons	Tho. & Benj. Godwin	Rhead & Goodfellow
Jno.! & Jas. Davenport	William Stanley	Machin & Co.
Thomas Heath	John Brettell	Wm. Bourne & Co.
Samuel Tomkinson	William Moseley	James Cartlidge
Ralph Johnson	Stevenson and Bucknall	J. and R. Blackwell
Thomas Bathwell	Wm. Walsh	Benj. Godwin and Sons
Edward Bourne	John Haywood	F. and N. Dillon
John & Christ. Robinson	John Wood	Ralph Stevenson
John Hall	Lindop & Taylor	R. and J. Clews

•,• Every Publican within this parish will be expected to keep one of these Notices conspicuously posted up in his house, as a proof he is determined to maintain good order therein.

TRAGOOTHILL, PRINTER.

Drunkenness, a long term problem for the industry, led to faulty wares and lost days. Many regularly pawned their meagre possessions to pay for drink. This 'tippling' notice was issued to publicans as a warning against supplying ale during working hours.

Alice Foxall

I worked in the glossed warehouse, the only place that would employ me at that age. When I was thirteen I started on handle making. We had to make 198 handles for three ha'pence. We rolled a bit of clay, put it in a mould, pushed the mould back and threw another up. When we'd made that 198 we took them down in the greenhouse to dry. That was repeated all day long, and we didn't get much money.

After serving about two years handle making I went apprentice handling. I had to put thirty six handles on for a dozen for which I was paid from two shillings to half a crown a week. I did this work until I was twenty one before becoming a journey-woman. I left the industry to work in Coventry during the First World War so when I came back again I had to serve two extra years before I could go journeywoman again. When your work was looked over, and some of it was broken, you got nothing for it. I can remember a time when I'd done some work that I should have been paid more for, but wasn't, so I didn't care how it was done. When the boss saw it he said, "That hasn't got to go through, it's got to be broke." I said, "Well I'm not breaking it, you break it." He said, "You've got to break it." But I wouldn't. There was a time when we had "good from oven" but then it was "good from hand". Well, him and me didn't, from this time, have much to say to each other.

I think I was only thirty-three when I had an operation and couldn't work until the last War started when I went back again. I found a lot of improvements had taken place. Your work was carried out for you, something they never did when I was an apprentice. I don't know who designed these factories but the handling house was up two flights of stairs. We carried a board on our shoulder right across the firm into the greenhouse. Many a time you tipped a board up, you couldn't help it, and there might be three dozen pieces on it, which was about an hour and a half of work. We had to stand that ourselves. One firm that I worked on if you went to the greenhouse and there happened to be two cups short on a board you had to take the board back up the stairs. You weren't allowed to go back for two cups, you took the whole board back up the stairs, but I never did.

We used to say things even when the boss wasn't too far away. If he had heard us he wouldn't have heard very good remarks about himself. But by and large the bosses weren't too bad to us. When we had to do the cleaning out we were told to scrape under our bench but we weren't allowed a sweeping brush because of the dust. It wasn't very pleasant because we also had to go and fetch buckets of water and carry them down twenty to thirty steps.

Sometimes we had a good laugh. I remember one instance when it was one of the cup handler's birthdays. She paid for port wine and eccles cakes. In the afternoon everyone was asking what had happened to Gertie. Eventually, when it was time for the port wine and cakes we found Gertie asleep under a bench minus the wine. Gertie never lived it down. We often laughed as hard as life was.

There was a family of us, four cup handlers and my father who was a placer. When he had to finish his job, through a misunderstanding, he had to stand on Hanley Market Square where all the placers were waiting for a day's drawing which, if they were lucky enough to get it, they got five shillings for. They needed five pairs of eyes because of the different districts the men came from. Bucknall Meakin's came up Bucknall Road and Parliament

Row, Meakin's and Johnson's came up Piccadilly, and Bishop and Stonier came up Lamb Street, and Weatherby came up High Street. When men saw someone coming they all dashed. They needed five pairs of eyes. Oh the disappointment. I saw my father once run for a job but he didn't get it. He was no chicken then and couldn't run very fast.

When I first started to work, to give you an idea what time I had to start out, I left home on a Saturday morning with father at five o'clock. We had to be there on Saturdays at 6a.m. When we were crossing the town father used to go in Wilder's wine bar for a rum which was tuppence. I would go in with him. There I would sit watching him with his little drop of rum, and there was a stove pot in the centre of the room and a big barrel. He'd put his glass on it, have five minutes and away we were, and I was at work long before six o'clock. We worked til one, and for that we got the large amount of half a crown.

When I got older I got ten shillings a week. I didn't know how to start to spend it, it was a fortune. You could go out at night for tuppence at The Grand. That was a good evening out. Four pence for the theatre, that was another good evening out. Your money went a long way. But if you weren't working you saw more dinner times than dinners. Of course the time came when you could get married. You were determined that your children weren't going to go in the industry, but there weren't any other jobs. During the Depression I can remember being on the dole. Some women got a list, a paper, and they took it round to the factories to show that they'd been after that job. They had to get it signed for the Dole to believe them.

G.W.E. You told me earlier about your wish to become a teacher.
A.F.   Yes. When I was at school I never brought a report home that wasn't good. It was suggested that I might go to Hanley High School, but my parents couldn't afford the books never mind the clothes. So I had to go on a factory. That was in Meakin's warehouse.

I worked there from January until the September. I can remember now that there were these great big meat dishes where I was working that I had to keep walking round. To save going round I just stepped on them and away. One day the boss followed me through and wondered who had put their feet on them. I didn't admit I knew or he would have sacked me. That was one thing I didn't admit.

We used to sit in a little place to have a meal, about four of us, all young girls. Before we went in the men, who were packers, sat in this place. Well, we sat there, and all of a sudden there came a great big rat down a pipe. I think we were too afraid to scream but it came up to us because the men had been feeding it. It didn't get anything out of us because we hadn't enough for ourselves.

It would have been nice if I could have gone into teaching. I would have had a different life than I have now. Before the Depression they were advertising for potters in America, and my father decided to apply. As I've said there were four sisters, all cup handlers, and my father was a placer. It was an excellent opportunity but mother was taken ill with pneumonia and so we couldn't. Then, of course, we carried on here. We saw the Depression through. After that things brightened up a bit.

G.W.E. Did you work on any other factory?
A.F.   Meakin's I worked on. When we were at Coventry all of a sudden my sister was taken

ill and she had to come home. I decided also to pack up and come home too. I got a job with Kent's of Longton. There was nothing about the place that was attractive. Meakin's was an open place but at Kent's everything seemed to be on top of us. It was not nice at all. When I worked at Meakin's I was close to the towing shop. Well, when the towers came out they would bang their clothes to get the dust out, dust they swallowed. I never again want to see anyone with silicosis, it was shocking. For months there was this girl who sat in one of those old armchairs, and there she died. Arthur Hollins was our M.P. at one time.[1] My father used to say he made one speech in Parliament but it was marvellous for us. He got silicosis classed as an industrial disease. Before then you didn't get anything - break your neck you still got nothing.

G.W.E. If you had reason to believe you were suffering from one of these industrial diseases was any interest or concern expressed by your employer?
A.F.   Not really. During the First World War I went to work at Jones's in Stoke. There they would send certain workers to the hospital if they complained of chest problems. There was a man plate-maker they sent who when he came back from the hospital said, "Doctor says there's nowt up wi' me, it must be the ale I've drunk that's swilled it all away." Perhaps it had!

Placers, when they had done a day's drawing, put a board down and lay on it, and the masters would bring them ewers of ale to replace what they sweat. Wherever a placer lay all round him would be the shape of his body in sweat because they were working near the ovens, which were white hot, never mind red hot. From Meakin's they used to go across the Bridge Inn with two ewers and they were filled at the boss's expense.

G.W.E. It is a well-documented fact that drinking amongst workers was a serious problem, especially for the employer.
A.F.   I had a friend who worked at Cotton's. Mind you she was older than me, but when she was young she remembered men would borrow their wages on a Monday and spend them on a day's drinking.

We could be fined for working dinner hours. When I was a girl the fine was thrupence. My father used to say, "They should fine yer all yer wages." He said, "Yer union fights to get yer better wages. By working in the dinner hour you're getting more money than they can work out for the time yer there." Believe me, the day we started to work father saw to it that we joined the union. We didn't like paying the thrupence but we had no other choice, father would have gone mad if we hadn't gone in the union.

G.W.E. How effective was the union?
A.F.   Well, not much. I can remember in the Depression they dropped our wages. I have a feeling we had a cost of living bonus, but I won't be too sure about it. Anyway the masters dropped it. When the union man came I said, "If they want to drop our wages why aren't we brought out on strike?" He said, "Look, of all the thousands in the pottery industry you're two thousand. You won't be missed." So we couldn't call a strike. The union wasn't effective in that way. They tried hard over industrial disease, and it was Arthur Hollins that got it through. He was a big union man. He rose to the top.

The same with lead. I don't know whether they got compensation for lead but a glossed placer and a dipping house worker had a pint of milk a day where I worked.[2] I don't know if it was general. They used to go up to the office for this milk. Every month they had to pass the doctor to see if they had lead poisoning.

G.W.E. Did you ever hear of anyone on the factory with lead poisoning?
A.F. I knew one that had lead poisoning. He didn't work on the factory that I worked on but his wife and sister worked with me. This man had lead poisoning, and his wrists and ankles were swollen.[3] He was a dipper. The only one that I really saw with an industrial disease was a woman. I can see her even today, who sat in a chair and she died in it.

G.W.E. What was this woman's job in the industry?
A.F. A tower. The tower would put a dozen plates on a whirler, and turn the whirler round. She'd then use a tool to take the rough edges off. All the dust flew everywhere. When a plate was made it was what we called green, and when it was towed it was white. It was when it was white that it created the most dust. On cups the handles dropped off like dead men if the wares were white. You knew you would have to stand them if they came back. Some firms had a cellar for storing and keeping wares damp but we never did. You weren't supposed to leave any cups overnight that we hadn't handled. So we used to, if we'd got any, put a few on one end of the board with handles, and a few on the opposite end and then cover the others up in the middle that weren't handled, and put them right at the top of the stillage. We would go up four steps, and then slide the board on with the edge of our fingers. But what broke that up for us was when placers were waiting for work they'd fetch a board out. They knew whose they were because we had our own marks. They'd tell us they'd fetched a board with the centre covered up, and no handles on them in the middle. So of course we couldn't do that any more. Sometimes you had a good lookerover. You see if your work was a bit white the handles sprung and you would need to seal round them with a trimmer like a crocheting hook. Well she would usually do that but if she was offside or hateful she'd have you round and you'd have to trim them up whether they needed it or not. So therefore we were losing money again.

G.W.E. In later years I believe it was the case that handlers applied handles that had been made by someone else. In your years in the industry I understand you made handles as well as applying them.
A.F. Well, after the War they couldn't get handle-makers so they couldn't get anyone to train as an apprentice handle maker. We were growing older and bound to leave the trade. So no handle maker meant no apprentices to follow. They then brought in cast handles made using a mould with twelve handle shapes in it. You put the top on it which had a hole in it - a hole about three inches in diameter. You poured slip in through this hole and let it set about half an hour, then you tipped that slip out, turned the mould over, left it a bit longer, and took the handles out. It made it that you could make your own handles but if you could get a good handle maker it was preferred because it made life easier.

G.W.E. You were not, I believe, allowed to stay on the factory after normal working hours. When did the working day begin and end?

A.F.   From 8am to half past five. At one time we worked til six. That was at a firm in Stoke. Their handlers used to climb the gate at night. They also worked Saturday afternoon and Sunday. They used to climb the gate. But if we were on the firm after half past five the gate was locked, and we had to stand under the lodge until the nightman opened it at six (pm) when he came to sweep the place.

G.W.E. In those areas on the factory away from the ovens was cold ever a problem, especially in winter?

A.F.   Well, there was always steam and pipes that ran under a stillage. The stillage was in the centre of the shop, and there was a handle that we turned if the pipes were too hot. This meant you were able to regulate the heat.

G.W.E. The reason I mention the business of keeping warm is because there is photographic and other evidence that workers stood in a box of straw to keep their feet warm.

A.F.   Well, some even during the time of the Second World War, wrapped newspaper round their feet. Some shops would have a stove pot.

One event I remember particularly well happened one day when I stood talking to a looker to the ware. As we were talking we overlooked the canal. While we were there a boatee came along and he was carrying a child by its pants as he'd pulled out of the water, and it was dead, a little boy about two or three. I'm sure I could describe the man now his face was so impressed on my mind. He was taking him to the mortuary.

Notes

1. Arthur Hollins was born in 1876 and entered the pottery industry before he was ten. For 20 years he was a handler at a Burslem factory. His career in the Union began in 1899 when he became treasurer of the Jet and Rockingham Association, and in 1901 he was acting secretary during the strike. For three years from 1903 to 1906 he studied chemistry and pottery at the Wedgwood Institute's technical school. From 1906 he was a Burslem Lodge delegate on the society's executive committee and became General Secretary in 1928. In the same year he became Labour MP for Hanley on the death of Samuel Clowes, his predecessor as General Secretary. He served as MP from 1928 to 1931, and from 1935 to 1945, and he was Lord Mayor of Stoke in 1933-34. He died in April 1962, aged 85. From F. Burchill and R. Ross *A History of the Potters' Union*, 1977.

2.   It is perhaps significant that a leading authority on lead poisoning, Dr Dowling Prendergast in his book *The Potter and Lead Poisoning*, 1898, makes no mention of milk in connection with the prevention of lead poisoning. On the subject of prevention he merely says: 'A good meal should always be taken before beginning their work, and the abuse of alcoholic liquors should be pointed out.' On the subject of treatment he writes: 'The medical treatment consists principally of prophylactic and alternative treatment. For the colic there is nothing to equal opium in full doses. The old fashioned mixture of brimstone and treacle is by far the best purgative for women and children.'

3   Mr. Cramp, H.M.s Superintending Inspector of Factories, identifies for the year 1896 the number of reported cases of lead poisoning as 631 being males 364 and females 267.

He states: 'The requirements of this section have brought to light some lamentable cases of great suffering from the effects of lead poisoning, such as paralysis of the wrists, fits blindness, deaths.

The dropped hand is caused by the paralysis of the extensor muscles of the forearm. The workman afflicted with it is more helpless, as he cannot lift up anything. It is the commonest form of paralysis met with in the Potteries.'

From *Cup and Saucer Land*
by the Rev. Malcolm Graham

Top picture, cup-handling.

Right handle making.

OPPOSITE PAGE:
Two more photographs from the book,
published in 1908

After original models in
Japanese porcelain. Moore
Studio 1905-1915.

King George V and Queen
Mary, accompanied by
Bernard Moore, on the
occasion of a Royal Visit to
the Potteries in April 1913.

Reginald Tomlinson
Ceramic Artist, Art Education
Administrator, Portrait Painter

Interviewed Chichester, 1977.

Almost all of the people who responded to my appeal for contributors were actually still living in the Stoke-on-Trent area, Reginald Tomlinson being an exception. Mr Tomlinson wrote to me from his home in Chichester to say that he had important evidence that would effectively rewrite a piece of local ceramic history. I was already aware of his reputation as a ceramic painter and designer, and especially his links with the Art Potter, Bernard Moore. Moore opened a studio at South Wolfe Street, Stoke-on-Trent in 1905. He had previously worked on a larger scale in partnership with his brother, Samuel Vincent at a factory in Fenton called the St. Mary's Works. The sudden death of Samuel at the relatively young age of thirty-eight forced Bernard to review his future, not least because it is said that his younger brother had been content to oversee the day-to-day running of the factory, an arrangement which left Bernard free to concentrate on his glaze experiments.

Since the middle years of the 19th century several potters working in France had set out to recreate the much admired Chinese glazes variously known as flambe, transmutation and sang de boeuf. They were in large part attracted by the mystery that Western collectors had learned to associate with such effects. Those glaze specialists who were successful in recreating the necessary glaze and firing technology were generally reluctant to reveal details of their findings. Moore responded to the challenge with an enthusiasm to equal that of his continental contemporaries. By the early 1900s he was confidently able to claim that he had perfected what he chose to call flambe. Moore was also making ruby and other lustres at the same time.

His studio only ever employed a small number of people, one of whom was Reginald Tomlinson. As explained in the interview to follow, like Reginald Haggar he moved into Stoke-on-Trent from the more congenial environment of southern England. His interview hardly disguises the fact that he never actually felt at home in the Potteries towns. Indeed, Reginald Tomlinson's art training and skills as a portrait painter were destined to lead him to greater things.

His decision to contact me was motivated by the belief that the credit accorded to Moore was misplaced. He claimed that a Moore employee named Edward Wilkes was in fact the man to whom we should attribute the rediscovery of flambe. With relevance to Wilkes's claim it must be said that attributing this particular discovery to anyone in Europe is always going to be problematic and highly contentious. The essential feature of copper-red glazes is what is known as a reduction firing. Reduction occurs when there is incomplete combustion of whatever fuel is being used to fire the kiln. This has the effect of creating smoky conditions in which the oxygen content is significantly decreased. Potters since antiquity had intentionally, and unintentionally, benefited from the properties of reduction. The Chinese are especially distinguished in this connection because they were able to reproduce it at will for novel effects. In the British ceramic tradition William De Morgan, to name but one, had drawn on the properties of reducing conditions in his creation of low temperature lustres.

In any attempt to undermine the status quo an argument has got to be well ordered and based upon sound evidence. What Mr Tomlinson describes amounts to conditions that would not lead to flambe effects. He says that Wilkes demonstrated his ability to recreate the glaze in a stove pot used to heat the studio. Unless the copper was suitably combined with a low temperature glass the characteristic features of the glaze would not have been created at what would have been a relatively low temperature. In setting his evidence against that known from other sources it fails to undermine Moore's pre-eminence as a flambe glaze experimenter, at least in the context of North Staffordshire.

This particular testimony proved to be interesting for other reasons. The Wilke's story on its own would not have qualified for inclusion because the main aim of my investigation was more concerned with issues surrounding the question of job satisfaction. I believe, however, that the Tomlinson interview was worthwhile in that it provided a unique insight into the workings of Moore's studio. His memories of Moore himself are also fascinating and important, especially those relating to his home to the south of the city, and his expertise in the then little known field of oriental ceramics.

Art potter Bernard Moore. A photograph that appeared in the *Transactions of the Ceramic Society* 1902-03. Following a period as an industrial potter Moore established a studio in South Wolfe Street, Stoke-upon-Trent in 1905.

Reginald Tomlinson

I was educated at Farnham where I was a boarder at the Grammar School, one of those old fashioned schools which are now, unfortunately, closed. We were fortunate in being in a district where they had a pottery kiln and the art teacher took advantage of the firing facilities which this offered. By chance I happened to do some good pots, and as it was known I was going to be an artist eventually of some kind, it was decided that pottery was my outlet. Friends of the family got in touch with Miss Hollins, the owner of Minton Hollins, and there they had recently appointed Gordon Forsyth who was really one of the first outside designers to be brought into the Potteries. He happened to be the travelling scholar in design from the Royal College of Art. It was extremely fortunate for me that I was put under his care.

When I went to the Potteries from Farnham I was astonished at the different surroundings I'd come to live in, and particularly interesting was the factory. I had never previously seen a factory. What interested me perhaps the most, and that stuck in my mind, was the fact that the painters at that period came to work in top hats. I know now that they were the last of what we might call aristocrats of the pottery industry, because they had studios to themselves. This was in 1909, many years ago. Things have altered very much since those days.

It was always my intention, although I was apprenticed as a pottery designer, to paint, and so I kept in close touch with the local art schools, starting at Stoke, and then winning a scholarship to Hanley. Many of the brilliant students from that school gained scholarships to the Royal College. I have in mind Charles Vyse, Harold Brownsword, men who have since made high reputations for themselves, particularly Charles Vyse, as an individual potter.[1] I very soon made up my mind that I wanted to follow these men to the Royal College, and was fortunate enough to eventually gain an exhibition scholarship which gave me ninety pounds a year maintenance, and three years in London, which was a very valuable experience.

Before I went to the college I had been appointed pottery painter and designer for Bernard Moore. I found a position there because I so admired what my trainer, Forsyth was doing at the Lancastrian Pottery. I was fortunate enough to get a similar position with Moore. Now, at that time, or previous to that time, Moore was turning out more or less repetitive type pottery. There was a fellow painter employed by Moore named Wilkes who spent his time painting prunus patterns but I introduced the individual type of pot that Forsyth was doing at the Lancastrian Pottery. I found Bernard Moore himself to be a most interesting character. He was quite eccentric. He would come to work with one stocking down or a piece of old tape tying up the other. He was a man of culture with a very intimate and deep knowledge of Chinese pottery of which he was a great admirer. Now Wilkes and I shared a studio and he frequently told me how hurt he was because he said it was he who discovered flambe not Moore.

I told him I found it very difficult to believe that a man like Moore would take the credit, but he insisted. In due course I said, "Well, if you are so definite about this Wilkes, prove it to me in some way." He said, "You know I've got a little pottery kiln in my kitchen at home, and if you are willing to buy me two pots, you can sign them, and I'll sign them, and bring back the results." He said, "You know from experience I often tell you how to get effects and Moore says, "Isn't it marvellous that that particular effect has come just at this particular part of the design." He thought it was accidental but Wilkes told me how to do it. This made me wonder whether he really had discovered it.

G.W.E. So Wilkes was an experienced all round practical potter and not simply a painter?
R.T.   He was a pottery painter. I asked him how if he discovered this how did it come about? Now, I knew we had, as they often had in those days, an individual fire in our studio, and he was always experimenting in the lunch break with some pot. This convinced me that he had a flair for experimenting. So I said, "Well, look how did you discover this?" He said, "One day in a lunch hour I was putting in a bit of china with some mixture on that I wanted to try out." He said, "I was doing this with copper oxide on a bit of pottery. It so happened that a piece of coal in this fire started blowing. You've seen gas blowing?" I said, "Indeed I have, I am always very intrigued." He said, "I put this bit of stuff in, and to my astonishment it went red. It should have been green, being copper oxide. I showed this to Mr Moore who said," "How did you do this Wilkes, tell me about it?" He said, "From that moment Moore developed flambe, and I've had no credit whatever, he has claimed the credit for having rediscovered Chinese red."

G.W.E. Did Wilkes give any indication of the date when this experiment took place?
R.T.   Well, it would be shortly before I went there, when he was developing flambe. I should say this was at least five years before the time we are talking about. Fortunately, I've kept these examples of his proof. They've convinced me, and for many years I've felt this ought to be made public. I know it's going to take a lot of credit from Bernard Moore but I think I should say that it was a mercy that Wilkes showed this to Moore because Wilkes wasn't in a position to develop it. Moore was a scientist, he was a cultured man with that background and was able to develop what has become, of course, a historic type of pottery. I think that should be said because I do sincerely feel that although he's taken the credit for being the discoverer he must be given the credit for exploiting it in the right way, in a cultured way.

G.W.E. So Moore never acknowledged any indebtedness to Wilkes then?
R.T.   You see I have so many examples of getting effects that Wilkes had told me to get, and Moore had said, "Isn't it fortunate that has just come where we want it." It could never have come where he wanted it if Wilkes hadn't said, put a little bit of so and so on that particular spot. It convinced me again that he knew more than Moore did about the possibilities of these colours.

G.W.E. Can you recall the conditions at the studio in South Wolfe Street?
R.T.   It wasn't a normal type of factory, it was really an artist's studio because it had a showroom, a kiln which no one was allowed to see, not even Wilkes was allowed near it. In the upper storeys were studios and offices, and the one studio shared by Wilkes and myself, and I worked with him that way for three years until I obtained a scholarship in

Bernard Moore's interest in single colour glaze effects was inspired by Chinese and Japanese porcelain. These Chinese examples date from the second half of the 18th century.

Bernard Moore flambe wares, based upon shapes in Chinese porcelain. Circa 1905.

London. Afterwards I got Wilkes a job at Crown Staffordshire. I was then Art Director there which is, as you know, now a subsidiary of Wedgwood. I persuaded the owner to engage Wilkes to produce some flambe, which I knew was very saleable. It didn't prove a commercial success at all so he was only there a few years.

G.W.E. So in comparison with the average factory it was a small setup?
R.T.   It was really a potter's studio, what you might call today an art pottery. Just an individual studio, mainly a showroom filled with the most delightful stuff, and a separate part at the back given over to kilns. Incidentally, we overlooked Spode.

G.W.E. How many people did Moore employ in those days?
R.T.   Oh, myself and Wilkes, that was the art side, the producing side really, and two girls. These were mainly occupied in producing plain pots, in red, no decoration. Wilkes and I were responsible for all the decoration. Incidentally, while I was there I was fortunate in gaining two international gold medals. Since I've got into the art world I've not met anybody else who's got international gold.   I got one at Caen and one at Turin for design in collaboration.

G.W.E. So that in those days you were part of a total staff of four or five people?
R.T.   That's all. It wasn't a factory you see.

G.W.E. Bernard Moore did the firing himself did he?
R.T.   He was the only one who fired. He wouldn't let anyone in the kiln room. I know now that he let gas in at a certain time. John Adams, Harold Brownsword and I were bosom friends, we were working to get to London together. Harold Brownsword was the son in law of Howson Taylor.[2]

G.W.E. You have mentioned the showroom at Moore's studio. Was this a showroom for trade buyers or were members of public allowed to buy direct from Moore?
R.T.   The public were allowed to buy. One of the great comedians, every time he came to Hanley's theatre, came down and bought some pots. Who was the little chap who dressed like a parson? He was very vulgar. He was very much favoured in the Potteries, and every time he came he went down to Moore's and bought pots.[3] While I was there King George V came and visited the showroom. I did a special pot for him.[4]

G.W.E. Did you actually meet the King?
R.T.   Oh no, old Moore kept us out of the way. I saw him over the staircase - the King and the Queen. Collectors were constantly coming from all over the country.

G.W.E. Were there people who came regularly?
R.T.   Yes. It was like a shop, in other words visited mainly by collectors and experts because his stuff was rare, wasn't it?

G.W.E. I suppose many of the pots made at Wolfe Street were one off pieces that were never duplicated?
R.T.   Yes. Many pieces were individual, especially our work. You see I wasn't a figure

man therefore my work was different from the normal. I illustrated *Omar Khayam* on big jardineres. They are in museums all over the world. I was fortunate because Forsyth was a figure painter. I did a lot of work of that kind.

G.W.E. It is said that Moore didn't make the pots that he glazed and decorated. Can you comment on this?

R.T. He didn't make any. He bought his pots from somewhere in Longton where I used to go and stand by a thrower while he did it. I said so much here..... take so much off there,

G.W.E. Can you remember which factory you went to?

R.T. No. I can only remember the man, the thrower. He was said to have been a prize thrower. He was once a mayor of Longton. I think you ought to know Bernard Moore was very well-known at the Victoria and Albert Museum. He made arrangements for me to go down to London and measure up the famous Chinese pots they had there. They were of tremendous value, and I very much valued the opportunity.

G.W.E. I take it the pots were biscuit fired in Longton and then delivered to or collected by Moore?

R.T. They were not only biscuit fired, they were fired to Bernard Moore's specification and glazed, and they were all white. They were all white-glazed with his own glaze recipe. All his pots came from this one factory. I regret I've forgotten where, although I went there.

G.W.E. Were there any exceptions to this arrangement?

R.T. All from this one place and to his own specifications.

G.W.E. I believe that you knew Bernard Moore on a social level?

R.T.   I stayed with him in the country, and I couldn't help comparing him with Gilbert of Sullivan fame because he had the same type of house that I've heard described. He had a pond in the garden which he used for swimming. I found them a very interesting and united family. Bernard Moore's brother died and he took on his family. He also educated his brother's family. A very cultured family they were by the way. Very different from what I imagined was the norm in the Potteries.

G.W.E. Would you say that Moore was well off in the material sense?

R.T. No. I would say he was comfortably off but I think he struggled to make a living from the pots. You know to keep up this place in Wolfe Street. I don't think he was a wealthy man but he did keep going a very nice country house. He had owned a fine pottery in Longton where the Moores made lamps with raised flowers, and he gave all that up to go over entirely to flambe.

G.W.E. The flambe ware is so very different to the things he produced in Fenton at his St. Mary's Works.

R.T. Oh, entirely different because of his obsession with Chinese art, and knowledge of it, a deep knowledge. I repeat he was a cultured man.

G.W.E. Was he a good man to work for?

R.T. Oh splendid. He gave me every opportunity, and he was the first man to allow me to sign my pots. Do you know my symbol? It's a beetle. That was quite a breakaway you know. No designer before my time ever signed their pots.[5] They were never given the opportunity but Moore, you see, appreciated that these were personal things, and by God it paid him because he got something which had a name on it. They were individual weren't they?

G.W.E. How long did you work for Moore?
R.T. Three years. It was so interesting because I knew what I was up to. I was trying to get to Kensington, and was taking all the necessary examinations but I didn't tell him. I think about a week before I heard I had got a scholarship to Kensington he got me to sign an agreement for so many years, at an increased salary.

G.W.E. So it wasn't your plan to make a career in the pottery industry?
R.T. I never intended to because I was a painter at heart. It proved right because I have made my living by it. If I may say so I've quite a reputation as a portrait painter.

G.W.E. So you left Moore before his studio closed?
R.T. Oh yes, a long time. As a matter of fact in the vacation, the Royal College vacation, I came up to Stoke and did exhibition pieces for him, special things you know, elaborate illustrative things. Most pottery painters were flower painters and I was a figure painter, trained by Forsyth. By God he was a good draughtsman.

G.W.E. I have heard a lot about Gordon Forsyth, a very influential teacher in those days.
R.T. He was a brilliant chap, a brilliant draughtsman. I've got a great admiration for him. By the way while I was at Bernard Moore's I had the great privilege of working with Professor Anning Bell on the sgraffito frieze for Birmingham University.

G.W.E. If we may return to the methods used at the studio. Was it customary to fire the flambe glazes at a much higher temperature than the lustres?
R.T. Oh no they were all done in the one firing. And by the way although one worked in great detail, it was like working with mud you know. It was a thick, brown muddy mixture.

G.W.E. Earlier you mentioned Wilkes. Was he older or younger than you?
R.T. Oh, much older than I was. I was a young chap. We worked side by side. He wasn't a great artist. Prunus was what he did well, on ginger jars. You've seen them, blue and white. He used to do that in flambe, day after day, and nothing else, and he couldn't do much else. But I dare say if he had had to paint some roses he would have been able to do it very well.

G.W.E. Did you live near the studio in Stoke?
R.T. I lived in digs up at Penkhull. I felt very homesick because I'm a southerner, and was at school at that lovely old place, Farnham. When I arrived in the Potteries I was shocked, very shocked. It shocked me you see. I had never seen any smoke or factories before in my life. There was a pall. It was a period when there was a definite pall always over the Potteries. In fact a long, black cloud. You've seen postcards have you, and it was really so. From Penkhull I looked down on a pall of smoke.

G.W.E. Did you find the people of the Potteries easy to get on with?

R.T.   It's an experience, believe me I'm very grateful for. Here was I protected in a lovely district, and I got it bang on the nose. The first thing they said was, "Thay'st a bloody fool to pay a premium to come here. You know what'd happen?" I said no, "They'll offer thee thirty bob a week when thee'st finished." Well, they weren't far wrong. They offered two pounds.

G.W.E. So you left Stoke in what year?

R.T.   I think 1912, to go to the Royal College. Then I had three years there, lovely, lovely life. That was a grand change. Imagine coming from the Potteries to London. Although we only got ninety pounds a year we managed you know. I had a little clothing allowance in addition but still we managed - amazing! Bed and breakfast then was twelve shillings a week.

G.W.E. Did you ever return to the Potteries to work?

R.T.   I did. The first job I got was at the Hague, before coming back to Stoke. I did the figures in the dome of the Palace of Peace. It was the first job I got after graduating from the Royal College. At the College there was an architectural section and two Dutch architects were on the course, and they saw that at the Royal College we were trained as mural painters. So we got jobs there. I got the job to do the figures up in the dome.

   I could see the end was coming to the job and I wrote to Reg Moore, who was Bernard Moore's nephew, and who was running the studio for Bernard Moore; one of his adopted sons. It was a good thing because he was a businessman, had a business head. I wrote and said, "I'm finishing a job over here and would like to come back if there is a post vacant." By God he wrote back and said, "Come as soon as you like." So I went back there.

   One of the girls in the showroom said that there had been a potter there asking Bernard Moore if he would allow me to go part-time to the Crown Staffordshire Porcelain Company, and Moore said, "Certainly not." He didn't ask me at all. This girl said, "I don't think it's fair to you that he should say no. They are offering you a big job." So I got in touch with them and said "what is this idea?" They offered me very good money in those days -a pound a day for as many days as I liked, which was very good. So I went to Crown Staffs and became their Art Director. The trouble was that I found I couldn't stretch myself there.

G.W.E. So you found the work there rather restricting?

R.T.   I was an experienced painter by then and I'd been to the Hague, and so to be doing pansies and forget-me-nots and roses was not very rewarding. I saw a post advertised for a painting master for Cheltenham. I said to the wife, "Look I've no opportunity to develop here what I want to paint." I said, "Are you game for me to apply for this job?" "Indeed" she said. "I know Cheltenham and Gloucester very well, lovely places." I got the job. In three years I was Principal.

G.W.E. What happened after that?

R.T.   I saw the Chief Inspector's job for London which was, in those days, £1500 a year. Do you know what that was then? I mean that was a prince's salary, and I got it.

G.W.E. What date was this?

R.T. It was 1925. To be Art Adviser to the biggest authority in the world, which it was. America had got lots of departments but nothing compared with London, 2,000 schools, 22,000 teachers -and I was Chief!

G.W.E. Did you stay in that post until retirement?

R.T. I stayed twenty-five years. They were grand people to work for. When I retired from this job I went straight over to portrait painting. First commission I got was the Chairman of London County Council. There isn't a better showroom than County Hall, London.

Notes

1. Charles Vyse 1882-1971 was born into a family of potters. He trained as a modeller at Hanley School of Art before obtaining a scholarship to the Royal College of Art where he also worked from 1905 to 1910. He later established a workshop at Cheyne Row, Chelsea. Vyse had a particular interest in the recreation of Chinese glaze effects. His studio was damaged by air raids in 1940 which led him to move from London, later becoming a teacher at Farnham School of Art.

Harold Brownsword studied sculpture at Hanley School of Art. 1908 awarded a Royal Exhibition: 1938-50 Principal of the Regent Street Polytechnic School of Art.

2. William Howson Taylor (1876-1935), contemporary of Bernard Moore, shared his passion for Chinese glaze effects. Richard Howson Taylor, his father,who was born in Burslem, Stoke on Trent, later left the area to become Head of Birmingham School of Art. William was an exceptionally talented Art Potter with a very detailed knowledge of high temperature glazes. In 1898 he opened his Ruskin Pottery in the West Smethwick area of Birmingham.

The name Ruskin was used as a tribute to the Victorian art critic and writer, John Ruskin. It is said he gained his initial experience of pottery making at his uncle's Howson Pottery in Hanley which, incidentally, was at that time under the artistic direction of the Edward Wilkes discussed by Reginald Tomlinson.

3. I am told by Ray Johnson that the 'vulgar comedian' referred to by Mr Tomlinson was almost certainly George Robey (real name George Edward Wade 1869-1954) who appeared on more than one occasion at a Hanley Theatre. His first stage appearance occurred in 1891, later securing roles in musical shows such as The Bing Boys (1916). He was knighted in the year of his death.

4. In March 1913 it was announced in the local press that George V and Queen Mary were to visit North Staffordshire on the 23 April. It is very indicative of Bernard Moore's growing reputation at this time that the Royal party would see only two potbanks in Stoke itself during their visit, namely that of Spode, and the studio of Bernard Moore. The visit, according to The Pottery Gazette, lasted for twelve minutes.

5. Although most employers refused to allow designers and artists to sign their work Reginald Tomlinson's claim that he was the first to be allowed to do so is incorrect. In the case of Minton alone artists such as Solon and Boullemier regularly signed their work.

The Royal Party leaving Moore's
studio following their visit to Stoke-
on-Trent in 1913.

Flambe vase by Bernard Moore,
circa 1910.
*By kind permission of The Potteries
Museum.*

Gordon Mitchell Forsyth, eminent
designer and educationalist,
photographed in the 1930s.

Lustre-painted vase by G.M.
Forsyth, Royal Lancastrian
Pottery, early 20th century.
*By kind permission of The
Potteries Museum.*

Mr H. Hulse
Works' Director

Interviewed Hanley, Stoke on Trent, 1974

Documentary evidence exists to show that from the early years of the 19th century it was not uncommon for the more enterprising amongst the city's potting community to amass sufficient capital to enable them to progress from the ranks of the employed to that of factory owner, if only on a modest scale. It was not always necessary that they had funds to enable the purchase of a potbank outright. Newspapers of the day contain advertisements detailing premises that were available on a lease. That many of these businesses proved to be shortlived is confirmed by checking the pages of, for example, Geoffrey Godden's *Encyclopaedia of Pottery and Porcelain Marks*. It was not unusual for a venture to survive for a mere three to five years. A business might fail if its continuance depended on the prosperity of a single or small number of retail outlets. Retailers, and indeed wholesalers abroad, often experienced a precarious existence from a variety of causes ranging from financial insecurity to civil disturbance, and even military invasion. There are well documented instances of recently established owners dying within a short period of setting up in business, often because they were approaching retirement age before being in a position to strike out on their own.

Apart from the need for adequate capital an aspiring industrial potter was required to have a sound knowledge of the full production process. The very nature of industrialisation was that it required workers to specialise in some particular stage of manufacture. Specialisation was obviously unconducive to obtaining a knowledge of practices outside one's particular sphere. Moreover obtaining a formal education in ceramic technology was, prior to the establishment of the North Staffordshire Technical College, limited to evening classes offered by the region's Mechanics' Institutes.

Joining a class of this kind was dependent on an individual's ambition. In other words formal training beyond the factory gates was not obligatory. The paternalistic structure of factory management was largely a result of these limited opportunities for a technical education. To this very day there are family owned businesses in Stoke on Trent where the sons of the proprietor have received their industrial training by spending an appropriate period in each main department of the factory.

Given an awareness of the above circumstances I was particularly pleased to be approached by someone - Mr H. Hulse - who had experienced personally going from being a wage-earning employee to factory owner, in this case as a partner with his father. Mr Hulse was also someone who had received some of his ceramic training under the tutorage of Drs Mellor and Scott at the City's main technical college, then situated in what is now College Road, Stoke on Trent.

A particularly interesting and unusual aspect of his experience was his employer's secondary business venture in connection with the running of a Longton theatre. He recalls how, at least on one occasion, a girl from the factory staff was released from normal duties to enable her to take on a role in the company's travelling pantomime.

Mr Hulse's case typifies what I briefly described at the start of this introduction, in that he progressed from the factory floor to join his father in setting up a new pottery venture. It was unfortunate that their decision happened to coincide with one of the most difficult periods in the industry's recent history, namely the General Strike and later the Wall Street Crash. He recalls having to sell their wares for 'rock bottom' prices and then spending an especially quiet period painting the outside of the factory. It was not until several years later that he was able to return to his former managerial status by working for someone else.

Certain items in the pottery manufacture, especially when they
involved high levels of skill, were dependent on many
contributions. This finely decorated vase from the Ridgway factory
was the product of a team of more than a hundred workers.

Mr H. Hulse

I joined the industry from high school in 1918, just before the end of the First World War. Originally, when I first started high school I was supposed to be going on to be a teacher. Teaching wages in those days were so terribly low that my father, who was in the pottery industry, suggested that I should start as a mould maker, with the objective of becoming a manager later. So I started as a mould maker on a china works, at the same time doing three nights a week at the technical school. In those days you started at Longton, and took the preliminary course. If you passed the exam you then proceeded to Stoke and took the final years, what they termed the Honours Course. That was as far as you could go. At that time Dr Mellor and Dr Scott were the two principals of the college at Stoke.

Anyway after two years mould making, and incidentally when I started there were only two apprentice mould makers because the men hadn't returned from the War. There was myself and another apprentice. I was bigger than him so they always looked upon me as if I was the head mould maker. Eventually the head mould maker returned from the War and I worked with him, and learned the trade with him for a while. Suddenly there came an opportunity for me to go as assistant manager on an adjoining earthenware factory, which was owned by the same company. So I took over the job of assistant manager. Now my duties were fairly onerous, and I hadn't a minute to spare any time in the week. My first duty was to count all the work carried out in the green house. As we'd got about twenty-four or twenty-five makers, and twenty-one cup handlers, that took quite a considerable time. It was all counted as it passed me on boards.

It's very interesting to see how the cups were counted. They were sent out in long dozens, and paid for at the rate of long score, that is 36 times 20. Now each cup maker would put on that board a little bit of biscuit pitcher with his initials on. Those went to the handler who was responsible for collecting them, to give him his count at the weekend else he got no wages. So every settling day there was usually some argument as to how many they were short, checks lost or handles wrongly counted. Anyway we usually managed to work it out in the end because don't forget they'd got to pay out their own attendants out of whatever they received. They had to pay the sponger and the mould runner. They were responsible for that themselves, and also the clay carrier had to be paid. The clay man went round every Friday night and collected so much per person. That was how he made his wages.

Another part of my job was to file the potter's profiles. That particular firm, which was Cartwright and Edwards of Longton, had three factories all within a range of a few yards, two earthenware and one china. Well, the manager I worked with, plus a manager from one of the other earthenware factories, had to do all the profiles for those three factories. For this we were paid thirty shillings, between us, not each, for the filing of profiles and keeping them up to date. The money was divided. The man over me got fifteen shillings, I had 7/6d, and the other manager had 7/6d. The top man had fifteen bob. Anyway it was quite a welcome addition in those days to our salary.

Incidentally, we worked a forty seven hour week, and that factory was fully self-contained. It had its own mill, alsing cylinder pans etc in the slip house. We even had a flint kiln because we calcined our own flints. So there was a good general knowledge gained from it. Another part of my job was to do all the mixings with the slip maker. The mill, where the blungers were, was over the mixing pot so it was run down from there, and we controlled it by ringing a bell when we wanted him to stop. I had the mixing to do, inches at so much per pint and so on. The means of communication was just an electric push button bell. That was another part of the job.

After I'd counted out all the work I put it down in their books and my book. Thursday was settling day and we paid out wages on Friday. Everyone had his own settling book. We had flat and saucer makers, cup makers, a jug jollier, two pressers, and a hand dish maker, plus three bowl makers. Two large ovens, biscuit ovens, were set in and drawn every week. They were among the biggest in Longton. It was drawing day Monday, set in Wednesday, drawing day Thursday, set in again Saturday. It was hard work. A regular team did their own drawing and setting in. I can see them now, good workers for very little money. The two pressers made all sorts of stuff, covered dishes and so on.

We had a tremendous lot of families working on that particular factory. One I can remember in particular was the hand dish maker, his wife who did his sponging, and his daughter did the mould running. Now, another peculiar thing on this factory was that the flat and saucer makers sponged and fettled their own work, they had no sponger or tower. This wasn't prevalent on many factories. When they got there in the morning the first job was to sponge and fettle the edge of every piece they'd made the previous day. Now, that was supposed to be done in a green state but naturally some of it had been lying about all night, and was white. They were not supposed to do them if they were white. This led to the dreaded silicosis. The majority, although we didn't realise it at the time, died before they were fifty years of age.

The factory where I first started, the managing director, and one of the other directors were the owners of the Longton Empire Theatre of those days. So, one of my duties, which I enjoyed, because I got time off from normal duties, was taking some of the artistes round the factory during the week. We had Marie Lloyd, Jack Edge, oh scores of other well-known variety artistes of that day. In fact the management, and the directors, produced a pantomime and toured it for about six weeks. We asked for volunteers amongst the young lady cup handlers, and one girl volunteered and did a tour of six weeks and came back to work afterwards. It was a bit of a change from the slog.

Another thing that I used to enjoy was to go with my father to Bakewell to buy in stones for the mill, the grinding stones. I looked upon that as a great day's excursion, to avoid the settling and counting and so on. Little things like that in those days helped us along.

Afterwards, my father and I along with several members of staff, 1924 I think it was, formed a company, a new company and we called it Unwins Longton Ltd. It had previously been Joseph Unwin. The approach to it was known as 'Dark Entry' and it was in Longton. Everybody knew it as 'Dark Entry'. It was a four oven factory that had been making earthenware, a lot of it for the colonies, underglaze decorated, brightly painted patterns which had gone out of fashion. The trade had just gone. As a consequence the factory was closed, so we had to convert it to just the ordinary run of the mill earthenware. I, at twenty-two years of age, was in charge of production, thinking I knew it all. So I got our mouldmaker to do some of his own modelling, he'd never done any before but I gave him the confidence to get a start at plain modelling and he did it. He always remembered me for encouraging him. Anyway, we were there during the 1926 strike. We started in 1924, then it closed down. This was a blow to us to start with. I spent the time painting the outside of the factory, that's what I did during the twenty-six strike (1926 General Strike). We had a lease until 1931. In the meantime the corporation bought the whole of the block, so at the end of the lease we'd no security. The firm was wound up and we started again in 1932, just my father and myself in a small two oven factory. But by now the competition had become so great, and the prices so low, for example, white cups a shilling a dozen, dinner plates 2/6d. a dozen. We found it impossible to start a new factory, and make it pay under these conditions. As a consequence in 1934 we closed, and I said, 'Never again will I go back to the pottery industry,' but I did. It's one of those things it gets you.

So after a period I bought a business, even doing part-time insurance collecting, and travelled miles on a bike to do it. I eventually had an offer from a firm I applied to for a job previously and they wrote back to me. I went for an interview and there were managers there from the exchange, waiting for a job with what we termed 'green cards' in those days. Anyway I got the job, starting back as assistant clay manager where I'd started twenty years previously. I carried on there for quite some time until a friend of mine, who was wanting a manager, came and asked me to take on this job at his factory as clay manager. So I was starting up again to grow.

Eventually I did my last twelve to thirteen years with the Alfred Clough group and finished up as works director of Royal Art Pottery.

Longton

Ware placers with saggars.
From the Reverend Graham's
Cup and Saucer Land.

Beating a saggar bottom or
base at Allied Insulators,
Milton, Stoke-on-Trent.
Photographed by the author,
circa 1975.

Mr E. Hosey
Pottery Labourer

Interviewed Hanley, Stoke on Trent, 1974.

The interview to follow is the shortest I have chosen to publish. This is because more than half of what was said related to a later phase of the contributor's working life when he left the ceramic industry to become a coal miner. This change of career is in itself significant in that Mr Hosey had not served any kind of training as a young pottery worker. The few pre-mining jobs he had involved clay carrying and other labouring duties. At the beginning of our conversation he mentions a boyhood experience in connection with saggar making. Being a mere seven years of age at the time he was clearly too young to follow this up with a proper course of training. Had the experience occurred at the then official school leaving age of thirteen his later career might have taken a different direction.

Like other contributors Mr Hosey experienced severe poverty at an early age. For example, he mentions his mother's need to pawn the family's basic possessions. Following the saggar-making incident he went after leaving school to work for a local brickyard. His description of the job, especially where he talks about its physically demanding nature, is very similar to the evidence offered by childworkers to Scriven and Baker less than sixty years earlier. Perhaps his description of himself as being 'a big lad' was ironically somewhat limiting in that his size would have been immediately apparent to a potential employer. In this context a person's size could be something of a disadvantage.

Of all the people interviewed he was the one who, with the exception of a brief experience in a saggar shop, found work in the ceramic industry to be devoid of any real compensating features. While several interviewees experienced periods of hardship and often found their work to be physically and perhaps emotionally demanding they were able to recall periods of fulfilment or pleasant experiences resulting from their working relationships with others.

In view of the similarity between what he encountered as a young brickyard labourer, and conditions known to have characterised brick production in the mid-19th century, I am prefacing his testimony with an extract from Baker's report:

"I consider the employment of children in brickyards absolutely cruel, and that the degradation of the female character in them, is most complete.

The employment of females as brickmakers in the south and west of England, is not nearly so extensive as it is in those Midland districts where iron works prevail, and where, in consequence, there is a perpetual demand for adolescent and adult male labour, so that very few (adult) males are to be found in the brickyards, particularly in the fire-brickyards in South Staffordshire, for example. Hence children of very early years are sent to the clay yards and are brought up amid scenes and conversations which are most demoralising. One may, in fact, scarcely recognise, either in the person or the mind and manner of the female clay worker, a feature of the sex to which she belongs. I have seen a boy of five years old, working among two or three and twenty females, being 'broken', as they call it, to the labour. In one case, a boy of 11 years of age was carrying 14 pounds weight of clay upon his head, and as much more within his arms, backward and forward, from the temperer to the brickmaker, walking eight miles a day upon average of the six days, and in another, a boy of 16 was carrying green bricks to the floor in the mould, weighing 14 pounds there, and 3 pounds empty, and walking eighteen miles a day on average.

I have also seen females, of all ages, nineteen or twenty together (some of them mothers of families), indistinguishable from men, excepting by the occasional peeping out of an earring, sparsely clad, up to the bare knees in clay splashes, and evidently without a vestige of womanly delicacy, thus employed until it makes one feel for the honour of the country that there should be such a condition of human labour existing in it. I questioned one such group in a brickyard in South Staffordshire as to how many of them could read, and found that only one out of twenty was so qualified, and out of the whole number she only had been to a place of worship on the Sunday previously, the whole of them being partially employed on Sundays, as well as weekdays in 'battening', 'turning bricks', or 'earthing the kilns'."

Removing the wooden mould from a saggar at Allied Insulators circa 1975.

Mr E. Hosey

I was born in 1899 in Audley Street, Tunstall. We lived in Audley Street until I was six or seven years of age, and we flitted into Watergate Street. While we lived in Watergate Street, on the opposite side of the street, there was a potbank, known as the George Street Pottery, which extended into George Street, the next street to Watergate Street. Now opposite our house was the saggarmaker's hole where he made his saggars. We used to go and watch him make these saggars through the window. Eventually we got friendly and it finished up with us making him a jug of tea, for his breakfast or his dinner which eventually resulted in going round through the double gates that he used to have to open to get his marl. A horse and cart brought his marl. We gradually got into his saggar hole properly.

I'd be about seven or eight years of age, no more, but I was a big lad, and I asked him one day, "Let me have a go at knocking a bottom for yer." He said, "Fair enough", so he got a piece of marl, the proper size, he knew the size, and he knocked it together for me. He put plenty of sand in the ring on the frame that made the saggar bottom, patted it for me then gave me the marl. By the hokey that was enough to keep lifting. He showed me how to start knocking it, and the process to carry on with, and so I carried on. I finished up and I really got a saggar bottom as good as his. He said, "I wish you were old enough to leave school and you could come and work for me." That was my first experience on a potbank.

Now after that things were bad and we were very poor, poor people were poor in them days, in the early 1900s. I remember there was five of us, five children, two girls and three lads. Me dad had appendicitis and had to go into hospital. He was in there seven weeks not a ha'penny coming in from nowhere, no parish pay, no insurance, no nothing in them days. My mother had to pawn the pictures off the walls, the sheets off the beds, even the chest o' drawers had to go into pawn. If it hadn't been for a kind old lady who was a neighbour, I don't know what would have happened, and that lady remained a good neighbour to us right on until we moved out of the area.

Well, when I was eleven years of age my elder brother and two elder sisters had both started to work, all working in the potbank, one went to Grindley Hotel Ware. She started work there for 2/6d a week, running moulds for a bowl maker. My elder sister went on the Grindley Woodland Pottery, running moulds for a cupmaker, and she also got 2/6d a week. Me brother, because he was a big lad, same as I was when I was young, went on Alfred Meakin's, the Royal Albert, running moulds for a ewer maker, and that was a heavy job. He got nine shillings a week. So therefore the finances of the family were increasing.

So we flitted from there to Lyme Street in Tunstall, further along Sneyd Street. It was when we lived in Lyme Street that I come thirteen years of age, eligible to leave school. I left school the day I was thirteen with my school certificate. I then went to Oliver's in Stanley Street, who was the Registrar, for a birth certificate, which cost sixpence, and which you had to have before you could start work. Went down to Thomas Peake's brickyard and got a job working for a quarry maker. My wages for working for him, from six o'clock in the morning to six o'clock at night was four bob a week. Believe me that job was hell. I used to be that tired at night that I couldn't sit at the table to eat a bit of food. I just wanted to get on an old wooden sofa we'd got and go to sleep. Me arms were raw with mauling the clay and me feet were raw with treading on a red hot floor we had to walk on, and the fire was under ''em. We had also to keep looking to the fires otherwise we couldn't get the quarries dried. Then when they were dry, just dry enough, we had to polish ''em with a knife and then in the afternoon we'd press them and put ''em on a staging, another staging, for drying with fire under it so they'd be ready for going in the oven, and that's what went on from May until October. In October they closed it all down, Peake's did, quarry making, ridge making, everything except roofing tiles.

That threw me out of a job, and that was a Godsend to me because I went and got a job at H & R Johnson's Highgate Tile Works the very next week, at nine shillings a week, and that was a fortune to me after having only four bob a week. I went turning the wheel for a man tile-maker who made inch thick tiles and special thickness tiles. I stayed there a while until the manager asked me if I'd go saggar carrying for him which meant that they'd got a tile shop upstairs where all the young women worked. I had to learn how to balance a saggar on me head, so that I could carry two, one on me head and one in me arms, up and down fourteen steps all day. Well for that I got an increase of 1/6d, that made it ten and sixpence. So I stayed there until I was old enough to think about going in the pit. I couldn't go in the pit until I was fourteen. As soon as I was fourteen I went up Chatterley Whitfield and I got a job.

Saggars, no longer suitable for use, were found throughout
the city serving various functions, like a garden wall.

Appendix 1
The Reports of Samuel Scriven and Robert Baker

Introduction

My interviews were part of an investigation to determine the extent to which improvements in working conditions had taken place in the ceramic industry of North Staffordshire over a period of some fifty years. A second aim was to gain an insight into the subject of what William Morris and his immediate contemporaries identified as 'the joy in labour'. In Morris's case it was almost inconceivable that anyone could achieve such a state in an industrial context. He believed that the creative instinct could only be satisfied in the context of a workshop where traditional craft skills underlay every area of the production process.

Job satisfaction, spiritual fulfilment or 'the joy in labour' is a state of mind that may arise from a variety of activities that constitute human experiences. It would be wrong to assume that it is a prerogative of work that we may conveniently classify as 'artistic'. It is equally misleading to assume that repetitive even mundane duties are by their very nature incapable of giving rise to job satisfaction; my interview with lathe treader Mrs Alice Morris being just one example to the contrary. I have actually heard ceramic designers express frustration at the absence of any opportunity for putting into production their more ambitious ideas. In other words their creative output was determined by the market for their employer's products.

It is very unlikely that Scriven or Baker ever considered the possibility that the average pottery worker might expect anything more from their contribution to the production cycle than a living wage and conditions that were conducive to a reasonable state of health. High on the Factory Inspectorate's agenda was the hope that their findings and resulting recommendations would ultimately lead to regulations that would benefit industrial workers whether in ceramic manufacture or some other industry. My investigations were of course far too retrospective to have any relevance to contemporary working conditions. At the time my primary concern was the preservation of memories. Their then limited applications is borne out by the fact that it was not until thirty years later that I decided to make them available to a wider audience.

Unlike Scriven, who was expected to interview a large cross section of workers located by his visits to the district's factories, I established contact with my contributors with the aid of the local press. Scriven also extended his interviews to include personnel from outside the ceramic manufactories and accordingly received contributions from, for example, local representatives responsible for imposing law and order, school and Sunday school teachers, and members of the clergy. Robert Baker's survey carried out in the 1860s relied to a greater extent on his own observations and reports submitted to him by people with an inside knowledge of the district's factories.

It is important to mention that reports by the Factory Inspectorate have been on occasions called into doubt by later historians. E.P. Thompson, for example, believed that some of them were restricted in their reporting by a wish not to offend the factory owners.[1] Having studied the Scriven and Baker Reports with an open mind I feel that their respective testimonies are fair, unbiased and objective. More than any other documentary source they provide evidence that is both fascinating and harrowing. In Scriven's case he interviewed pottery workers from across the age range and from most branches of the industry, the majority limiting their respective contributions to a brief description of their duties, state of health, brief family details, and in the case of the children interviewed, the treatment they received at the hands of supervisors and immediate family.

Although both reports have been cited by subsequent historians, Baker's has been less frequently mentioned. I nevertheless feel that it provides an appropriate sequel to my interviews carried out a little over a century later. Some of the people I met obtained their first experiences in the industry less than fifty years after its publication (1865).

The section to follow consists in the first part of a sample selection from the testimonies of people interviewed by Samuel Scriven in 1842. A full transcript would have proved too lengthy, and some of the interviewees provide very similar experiences to those presented by others. In the case of the Baker Report, with its narrative format, I have included substantial sections as they appear in the original version. The brevity of most of Scriven's interviews was probably as a result of them being made in the contributor's place of work, and possibly taken down in long hand. The longer interviews were provided by the factory overseers and contributors outside the industry, and submitted in a manuscript form.

Notes

1. E.P. Thompson, *The Making of the English Working Class*, Penguin, 1963.

Second Report of the Commissioners
Trades and Manufactures Vol.1.
Printed by William Clowes and Sons, London, 1843.

Reports and Evidence from Sub-Commissioners, 1842. Samuel Scriven

Boyle Factory, Eldon Place, Stoke.
Proprietors Messrs Minton

Turning Room, T. 60, open air 44.

No.3, Lydia Dale, aged 20:
I have been employed 6 years this Martlemas, can neither read or write, attended a Sunday school a little, not long, at Stoke Methodist Connexion, can do needlework and knitting, not married. Always worked in this room as a treader or lathe turner, come at 6 to 7 leave at 6, the work agrees with me, have got good health and a good colour, get about 7s. or 8s per week, but the amount depends on my industry, as we are paid by the piece, and, as I help the turner, I get 4d to every 1s he gets, we sometimes together turn 40 dozen, such as egg cups, which are sized at 12's, teacups are sized as 36's, basins 24's, and so on. I am allowed half an hour for breakfast, 1 hour for dinner, out of the 12 hours. I live 4 miles from the works, get my dinner at the works, have father, mother, and brothers, but none are potters. Like the work pretty well.

Painting Room, T. 62, open air 42.

No. 11 Hannah Barker, aged 40:,
I am a widow, and managing the children in this room, have been employed in the painting department more than 30 years, have been employed by Messrs. Minton and Boyle 3 years. I come to work at 7, and leave at 6. I work with other women over times, always work by the day, and when we work over time get extra pay: l0s.6d. per week is our pay, but for working over time 12s. The children do not work over time, have about 16 girls in this room, 9 of them under 13 years of age, all of them are healthy now, but I have buried many out of this room, the smell of the turpentine and paint, and the closeness of the room, often occasions illness, it has never affected me. I began as early as most. Some of the girls can write, about 6 of them, all of them can read, all of them attend Sunday schools. They are very clean, and moderately well conducted. All of them do not go home to breakfast, the half hour allowed would not enable them to do so, as they live at some distance. Most of them go to dinner. We have holidays, about a month altogether in the year. I think they live pretty well, and have what is sufficient for children. From my experience I think that the children who work are better off than those who do not, it must add a little more to the common stock, the children under my care are better conducted than others in the same works because I watch over them with the eye of a mother, and teach them their work. In other rooms girls are mixed up indiscriminately with the boys and men, and I think get bad

A contemporary Victorian illustration of a government
factory inspector taking evidence from child workers.

habits, some are very good, but others you cannot subdue, we are very fortunate in these works, and seldom have bad characters here. Our masters would not permit it, they are nice gentlemen, and are very good to them. Mr Boyle goes round the works every day, there are not many of such superior characters as they are. I have 6 rooms under my charge, in all containing 70 women and children of all ages, their duties are the same, all paint, and my observations as taken down apply to them. There is also a man who superintends some of the work, who with 2 gilders the only 3 that are in this department, all are married men, and of correct characters. You will hear disastrous tales elsewhere, for I have witnessed myself a good deal of it in my time, some families have only 5s. or 6s. a week to support more than as many persons. I hope this may be the worst place you visit, but I fear it will not, as this is now the most prosperous part of the potteries. I know of one family living near me of 8, the man gets 6s. per week, the woman came into me last Saturday, and I asked her how she lived: she said that with the 6s. she bought a stone and a quarter of flour and a peck of potatoes, this lasted till Thursday night, then with 1s. she earned by washing she bought a brown loaf for 6d. and another peck of potatoes, which would do again till Saturday. Don't know how she paid the rent, in Hanley there is plenty such.

Inspector's comment

An intelligent woman, and appears to manage her department well. The rooms are clean, but want ventilation.

Minton and Boyle's factory was one of the region's most important by virtue of its size, hence 'quarter mile Minton', and the quality of its products. Herbert Minton was, at this period, probably more receptive than most of his manufacturing contemporaries in the industry to the adoption of any innovation that he thought would improve production. In the early 1830s, for example, he introduced the recently invented tile-making press patented in 1830 by Samuel Wright. He also commissioned, on a regular basis, eminent outside designers to produce new patterns for tiles. Augustus Welby Pugin and Owen Jones* were invited to submit tile drawings, and he put into production parian statuary after models received through the Art Union.

　　Although rather less is known about the working conditions on his factory it is safe to assume that they were, as claimed by Hannah Barker, significantly better than would have been found on most other factories in the area.

*The Grammar of Ornament, 1857 was perhaps his best known work.

Scolloping House.

No.19 Mary Vyse, aged 27:

I have been employed in this firm about 14 years, all the time in this department, I am married and have two children. There are only two of us working in this room, the other a woman. We receive the ware from the turners and saucer makers, and pass it to the handlers, or, if not necessary there, to the green house, to further dry. We have very good health here, the temperature is comfortable.

Despite evidence indicating above average working conditions at Minton's certain processes were inherently dangerous because materials and technology were not sufficiently advanced in the 1840s to provide an alternative to lead for earthenware glazes. The true leadless glaze was not to fully materialise for another fifty years. In china production it was possible to formulate a glaze without the need for lead oxide.

This interview also inadvertently reveals a characteristic of the factory system that channelled people into particular specialisms, and hence knowledge of processes that lay outside their particular area of responsibility. This meant that workers were often unaware of the properties of many materials to which they were exposed on a daily basis.

Dipping or Gloss House. T. 62, open air 48

No. 23, George Corbishley, aged 37:

I have worked as a potter 25 years, as a dipper 6 years. There are two rooms in this department, and 4 persons working in them: 3 adults and one boy (15). We receive the ware to be dipped or glazed from the scourers and biscuit warehouse. We carry it, after it is dipped, to the next room, where there is a stove, to be dried, and then into the sagger room, to be packed for the second process of firing. Nobody else dips but me. I am not paid by the piece, but receive 5s. a day, this is reckoned the worst work on the premises, and I am therefore paid better for it. Have never suffered in health yet, have known many others suffer, they get their limbs drawn, and lose the use of them. My hands are constantly in the mixture, don't know what the mixture is made of, they don't tell us, think it is not so bad as it used to be.

Inspector's comment

This room is spacious and, as well as the adjoining, has means of ventilation.

Although ware painters were regarded as being among the aristocracy of the skilled. Their work could be dangerous due to the turpentine vapours that accompanied the process of onglaze enamelling. Groundlayers also enjoyed a high status, and were paid in accordance with their skills and standing. As with the earthenware dipper, higher pay reflected the job's potentially injurious nature. Enamel painting could also expose workers to the arsenic content of certain colours. It was possible for someone to be directly exposed to this highly toxic chemical in instances where they practised wetting pencils (brushes) with their lips and tongue.

The following interview with fifteen year old William Briant is interesting in that he revealed to Scriven the information that although being able to 'read a little' he was unable to write. This admission is rather out of keeping with his job because he also mentions an ability to paint 'crests'. If in using the word crest he is referring to coats of arms, a particular speciality of the Daniel factory, it more than implies that he was able to add mottoes where applicable. It is, of course, possible that he was responsible for a particular part of the crest that did not include letters or words.

Mention of being 'allowed to do a bat or two' identifies the creative aspect of his ability. There are indeed in existence examples of enamel painting on small slabs or plaques, usually of porcelain. Paintings on plaques might depict a floral study, landscape or even a portrait, and may represent an aspect of a factory's official product range or the private work of an individual artist or decorator. Their production has continued to the present day. The majority of 19th century examples are the work of adult employees some of whom enjoyed a distinguished reputation e.g. Thomas Steele, Thomas Pardoe and Daniel Lucas. In the case of enamel painting we come closest to identifying an area of the ceramic production process that offered the employee the potential for artistic expression.

Messrs. Daniel & Sons, China Factory, Stoke

Painting and Gilding Room.

Men and Boys. T. 68, open air, 32. No. 57. William Briant, aged 15:
I have been with Mr. Daniels 1^1/2 years, am apprenticed for 7 years, get 1s. a week for the first year, and increase it 1d. a week for 3 years, then get half price for what I do to the end of 7 years. There are 4 of us working in the same room, and 11 men, our duty is to paint crests, flowers, and figures on the ware. I do not find the work hurt us much, but feel the confinement most. We do not work every day, sometimes have only 1, 2, 3 or 4 days in the week, if we have no work to do, we stay at home. I can read a little, I can't write, I don't go to school even when I don't go to work, because we don't know what work there is to do till we come to see, and then wait 2 or 3 hours before we find out. I go to Sunday school at Ebenezer, Newcastle. I live at Newcastle, we have no rewards for good conduct, except being allowed to do a bat or two, and take home to frame, we have very few punishments. I never get strapped, when we do wrong we have a good talking to, they never stop our pay, excepting when we are idle and don't work. I don't go home to dinner, always bring it with me and take it in the painting room. I am allowed an hour for breakfast. I come at 7, and go home at 6.

Daniel & Sons were well-known for the high quality of their enamel painting and gilding which they used to excellent effect on dinner services commissioned by the nobility and gentry of the day. However, the quality of their products was in no sense indicative of a well ordered system of production or an environment conducive to the manufacture of high quality products. Scriven's description of their works highlights the dilapidated state of its workshops.

Inspector's comment
The proprietor of these works, Mr Daniel, is 78 years of age, and commenced business 60 years ago. The premises are not very extensive, but there is a good business carried on, and 240 hands employed. It is situate in the lower part of Stoke parish, between two canals, and is well drained. The rooms and buildings are old and dilapidated, small, close, dirty, mostly damp and uncomfortable, never or rarely whitewashed. The painting, store, and showrooms are very good.

Unlike the heavier industries of coal mining and engineering ceramic manufacture provided jobs for the whole of the family. There is documentary evidence to show that employers outside the Potteries towns occasionally diversified their business interests in order to attract a key worker while at the same time being able to offer work to a man's immediate family. Professor T Ashton (*The Industrial Revolution* 1760-1830) has this to say on the subject:

'When an employer sought to engage a man from another district he often failed because he was unable to offer work to other members of the family. To surmount this difficulty ironmasters like those of Blackbarrow, sometimes set up textile works near their furnaces so as to provide employment for the women and children. Conversely, when an employer like Oldknow or Grey, wanted juvenile or female labour, he was sometimes obliged to extend his operations to agriculture, lime-burning and so on in order to find work for the men. The industrial unit was often not a single establishment but something approaching a colonial settlement.'[1]

In the interview with Thomas Shelly at Zaccariah Boyle's he mentions that all of his six children are engaged in potting.

Office.

No.74. Thomas Shelly, aged 69.
I have lived all my life in the potteries, and have had a good opportunity of observing the present and past condition, both morally and physically, of the children employed in them. I served my apprenticeship with a Mr Booth for six years, and got then 2s.3d. per week the first and second year, rose 6d. per week the third and fourth years, and then worked piecework. Provisions were cheaper then than they are now. I was then a presser, and continued in that department till I was 24. I then, with two or three brothers, commenced china-making, which was in its infancy, and was obliged to give it up in two or three years, from misfortunes. From that time I became a foreman to the late John and Edward Baddley, in Shelton, then to Messrs Meyer and Hollands, then to Zaccariah Boyle, where I am now. I do not observe any difference in the mode of carrying on the business of the trade between the present and former times. The men, women and children get about the same amount of wages, supposing them in full work, as formerly. There are not so many hands employed then as now, for the reason that there are not so many potteries. We have now 80 men, 39 women, above 21 years, 57 men, 56 women, under 21 years, and 6 boys and 7 girls under 13 years of age, now working more or less number of days in the week. Some do piece, some day work. The apprentice girls and boys are hired by the master. Some other boys such as saucer, plate, and bowl-makers, are hired by the men, and do not come under our control or management at all. I cannot tell how many rooms we have for working in, they are all so in and out. There are seven biscuit and gloss ovens, and one enamelling oven. The warehouse is lit with gas and candles. The rooms are small and low, but you must take them as they were built. The premises lie low, and in wet weather are very swampy, they are drained by sewers. I do not see much the matter with the children in regard to their appearance. Some of the occupations of the children are very pernicious, those, for example, in which lead is used, they are not so bad now as formerly, there is not so much lead and arsenic used. I have seen some bad cases in my time, they were, lameness in the hands and arms, pains in the bowels, and the like. I have children (six living), four as potters, two painting and two pressing. I would not bring up either in the dipping or scouring house, because I think it pernicious, and it would shorten their lives. I think the children generally read, some of them write, they mostly go to Sunday school, but rarely to day school, the parents cannot afford in many cases to send them, the times are bad just now, and have been for a year or two. In some instances their absence was attributable to the vice of drinking in parents, but I am happy to say that teetotalism has produced a moral change in their habits, and hope the children will reap the benefit of it.

Inspector's comment:
Mr. Zaccariah Boyle's works are situated in the lowest part of the town of Stoke, and is low and damp. The workrooms are of the same character as most of the rest, namely, small, ill-ventilated, close, and unceiled (sic). It is one of the oldest in the potteries, and, having been

added to as occasion required, is without arrangement as to departments, there being one of each kind, or more, here and there.

In my interview with Reginald Haggar he criticizes the Gladstone Museum for being too tidy. In its defence it must be said that were they to conscientiously recreate the poverty and squalor as witnessed by Scriven and Baker the museum's officials would not be allowed to admit the public. Few people alive today in western Europe have experienced working, on a daily basis, in flooded workshops which depended for their illumination on daylight and candles. Where Thomas Shelly claims not to know the extent of Boyle's factory was he indirectly steering the factory inspector away from workshops that were worse than those already seen or indicating the premises' warren-like arrangement?

Scriven invited written comments from several members of the local clergy. Without exception their lengthy reports concentrate on the profligacy that characterised many amongst their respective parishioners. Several other witnesses from the period report a catalogue of problems ranging in seriousness from criminal assault and robbery to widespread drunkenness. The people who suffered most from these activities were the perpetrators' wives and children.

The two concluding testimonies which follow were from the Incumbent of Cobridge, Thomas Redall and Inspector of Police, George Ryles.

Letter from Incumbent of Cobridge No.232, Rev. Thomas Reddall:
Sir, Feb.13
My connection with the district attached to the church of which I am the minister has been so recently formed, and my means and opportunities of acquiring information respecting it have hitherto been so confined, that I fear I cannot furnish you with any intelligence that will be of material importance to you in the prosecution of those interesting enquiries to which your time and energies are devoted. Brief and contracted, however, as it must necessarily be, it may probably serve to give additional force to the correctness of that information which you have already succeeded in acquiring, and as such I freely give you the benefit of it. I must candidly confess that I think the state of morals in this neighbourhood to be of the most alarming and appaling kind. Indeed, as far as my experience has enabled me to judge, moral principle is a thing, generally speaking, unknown! totally extinct - I mean among the lower classes, adultery, fornication drunkenness, and every species of vice and profligacy are practised to an extent that is awful to contemplate: and yet those who are living in the constant indulgency of these vices are not, or seem not to be sensible that they are guilty of any moral delinquency. Sir, the cause of all this evil can only be counteracted, this awful state of things can only be remedied by giving the rising generation a good, sound, and religious education during the period of childhood and early youth. The present and each preceding generation have not been properly educated, in early years they were not sent to day schools, and they seldom in after life frequented any place of public worship, the natural consequence has been what we daily witness, that having grown up almost in a state of nature they live, in the grossest ignorance and in the unrestrained indulgence of all their evil appetites and passions. You must, Sir, have ascertained, during the progress of your enquiries, that the children of the poor are put out to work at an early period of life, many and grievous evils, both to the

children and parents arise from this sad practice. Take a family consisting of father and mother and six children. In many cases the children will earn almost enough to support the whole family, and whatever the parents gain besides is generally spent at the alehouse, thus the parents' means of vice are increased at the expense, if not the destruction of the physical health and strength of their children. But the consequences to the children end not here: being put out so early to work they are necessarily deprived of that education which is absolutely essential to them, not merely as members of civilised society, but as candidates for a blessed immortality, nay more, they imbibe with the very dew of their youth the poison of ungodliness and infidelity, they breathe all the sweetness of their childhood in an impure and deadly atmosphere, they are nursed in vice, they are schooled in every species of immorality, so that at the age of 12 or 14 they are, both boys and girls, the most finished profligates, they are as it were grey-headed, if not in practice, at least in the knowledge of wickedness.

No.237: Mr. George Ryles, aged 47, Inspector of Police:
I am the Inspector of Police for the parish of Burslem. Have held the appointment 10 years last September. I was directed to call on you to furnish any information that it was in my power to give, bearing upon the subject of your inquiry, by John Ward. Esq., the high constable or chief constable. I have lived all my life in Burslem, was born in it. The nature of my occupation, during the first period of it, was that of a printer, afterwards that of a police officer. I am thoroughly acquainted with the practices of the workmen in the several departments of potting and of the nature and extent of the employment of children. The paper-cutters are little girls from nine to 14 or 15 years of age, who come to work at six in the morning, occasionally at four and five, and first begin by making up the fire, clean the shop, get coals in for the day, get out the ashes, broken ware, and things of that sort, some of them fetch water for the use of the room, and for washing ware, on these occasions they have a great deal to carry, as one man in a printing room would require at least 16 gallons a day. They are allowed half an hour for breakfast, which some bring with them, others go home. They are standing close by the transferrer, or on the move to and fro the room from the time they arrive to their leaving, except at meal times. In instances where they meet with cruel masters their occupations are very laborious. They are allowed an hour for dinner, but seldom or ever exceed 40 minutes, and very often not 15, in taking it. That which is considered the time for giving over is six o'clock, but if the trade requires it they work up to seven, eight, and sometimes nine o clock, sometimes they are not well treated, in many cases the women transferrers send them out on their errands, necessarily occupying the time of the child, who, on her return, has to fetch it up by hard labour, rewarded oftentimes by the printer with a flogging, blows, or hard words, or cursing. In printing rooms there are often four printers, eight women and four children. They are not particular as to their language and manners, whatever is going on is frequently caught at by children of tender years, vices soon take root, nature has entailed that upon us all. For boys, I look upon it that those who attend on the plate, saucer, and dish makers, are the worse schooled in the whole trade of potting, with the exception of oven boys. In general there are many boys together in a room with, perhaps, half the number of men or more. My reason for saying

that these departments are the worst schools is that the men, their masters, are of the lowest order. These boys come in the morning to work at six o'clock, get their scraps of clay out, sweep the rooms, and get in coals for the day, and carry out any portion of the master's work completed on the previous day, to the green house, or to the kiln, or to the oven, to be placed in saggars for firing. They then begin running moulds, turning jigger, or assist their masters in fettling the work off. They often come to work at five or half-past. Whenever their masters have neglected their work in the early part of the week (and that is a common occurrence) they then have their boys at work at four, and I have known them to begin at 3, they are allowed half an hour for breakfast, and an hour for dinner, for the same reasons the masters, as before stated, require them invariably to work during the meal times, and continue them up to eight and nine o'clock at night, else their hour would be up at six. Some of these masters behave very cruelly to them. I have known repeated instances when masters who have been drinking the day or two days before, come to work under the effects of drunkenness, and when they want a relish, such as a red herring, or something sharp, as vinegar and ham, sent these children out to beg for it off any neighbours, or to commit petty thefts in the market-place at the stalls, to gratify their appetites. I know these things of my own knowledge, and speak as a police officer, as well as in the character of an operative. I'll give you and example. A child of nine or ten years of age was taken up for cutting or breaking off a water tap and lead pipe. I found that this child had been instructed by his master where to find it, and bring it to him. He afterwards directed him where to dispose of it, and return to him with the proceeds of the sale: the child was committed for trial. At the trial I stated to the chairman at quarter sessions that I had reason to believe he was instructed by his master. The child was sentenced to three days imprisonment. I afterwards ascertained that my suspicions, as it regards the master, were correct, but nothing was done with him.

It was only this very day that an instance occurred of a girl who came to beg beer of the landlord at an ale house for her master. I could give you many proofs of what I say to be correct. I have seen little children hanging about stalls, only waiting opportunities to pilfer, and when they have succeeded run away delighted to take their prize back, and soon return again for the same purpose, not looking upon the act as criminal. I have known instances of personal cruelty exercised by these men towards their children, and have heard them cry for mercy many times. What I tell you now I am prepared to prove, it is not hearsay evidence, but evidence that I can substantiate at any time. I cannot give you the dates of any cases of cruelty coming before the magistrate, but they have occurred. I often hear mothers complain of the long hours of labour of their children, but they have no remedy. If they take the children away they would have difficulty in getting places again. My duties require me to be abroad of an evening: I meet a great many lewd women, and have often had them up for being drunk, and making use of indecent language in the streets. There is a deal of prostitution carried out in the factories, especially among the treaders and throwers, there are nevertheless as virtuous women to be found there as in the world again.

Report: The Justice of the Peace, November 11, 1865

The pottery districts proper are of considerable extent and very populous. The total area in acres of Newcastle-under-Lyme, Wolstanton, and Stoke upon Trent, over which this population lies scattered, appears to be 50,887, the inhabited houses in 1861 were 29,707, occupied by 75,806 males and 74,425 females, altogether 150,231, or 5 to a house.

The places more familiarly known as "the Potteries", are Tunstall, Burslem, Hanley, Shelton, Penkhull with Boothen, Lane End, Longton, Fenton, Sneyd, and Rushton: and they extend into three parishes, namely, Wolstanton, Burslem, and Stoke, which latter embraces the principal part of the whole number of places.

For my present purpose I am desirous of separating the potteries into the five subdivisions for which I have appointed surgeons, i.e. Tunstall, Burslem, Hanley, Stoke, and Longton, and their adjacent neighbourhoods, because it is with these subdivisions that I shall have mainly to deal in the following observations.

The Factory Acts Extension Act received the royal assent on the 26th July, 1864, and after assisting to prepare the necessary abstracts for your approval, on the 16th of August I went to the potteries, having taken residence there for a few months, under the conviction that, after all that had been previously advanced by the advocates for the Factory Act, or for the Mining Act, or for no act at all, and after the final adoption of the Factory Act with such modifications as would provide for a gradual introduction of its clauses, if I wished to make it a success, it would be needful that, for a while, I should live there. Because, first of all, I had to endeavour thoroughly to understand the pottery system myself and secondly, it seemed essential I should be present with the authority of my office and experience, personally to reply to questions put by anxious inquirers with respect to the anticipated interferences with a hitherto unrestricted labour, to allay fears, to suggest improvements, and to bring about conformity with the law by a gradual introduction of its provisions. Thus I hoped, neither, on the one hand, to re-excite prejudices, nor, on the other, to compel pecuniary sacrifices which were unessential to the protection of labour to the education of the young, or to the measures of ventilation and cleanliness in the places of work, and yet to adopt the most likely means of eradicating, or at least of materially diminishing, the diseases incident to a potter's life. On the 17th of August I called on Mr. Hollins, the senior partner of the house of Minton & Co., and the president of the chamber of commerce, who, with the utmost courtesy, went into the consideration with me of the readiest mode by which I could convey my mission to the master potters, and suggested that we should at once see the secretary of the chamber, because the chamber being composed of master potters, that circumstance alone, would afford me an excellent opportunity of explaining anything which it might be thought desirable to ask me. This interview with the secretary terminated in a meeting not only of the chamber, but of the master potters as a body, to which I was invited, and which was largely attended, and was in every way satisfactory. The result thereof I have previously had the honour to communicate to you.

From the 16th of August to the 15th of December, with the exception of two or three days now and then, I was resident in the potteries, visiting most of the "banks", endeavouring to understand the points on which the act was likely to be brought to bear, making myself familiar with every standard of excellence in the construction of premises, stoves, offices, ventilation, and cleanliness, the social or improvident habits of the people, the amount of school accommodation to be obtained, and the readiness with which it might be adopted if needful. And it was well for me that I was able to argue from the past, for with both masters and men, I met again with precisely similar observations to those I had had to combat in the textile districts thirty years before. I might, indeed, have been talking again with the same generation. Every old argument about the "act not being suitable to the trade", of "there not being children enough in the district for two sets", of "the difficulty of schooling those that would be employed on account of their dresses", and of "the loss of wages by full time reduced to half time," was repeated again and again.

The habitual drunkard, I was told, laughed at the idea of being coerced into temperance by the force of circumstances. Many of the masters, helpless in discipline, and defenceless as to control over their works, because but for a few years they were potters at the bench themselves, and had not yet learnt the position into which their enterprise and prudence had lifted them, shook their heads and "hoped that the strong hand that had been so long wanted had come at last." With a few among them the act was barely an idea, the benefit of which they were unable to appreciate. They found it difficult to comprehend that educated workers could be of more value to them than uneducated ones. And as to the workmen, some of them saw in the slightly advanced rate of wages which they were sure, they said, they should have to pay for older hands, only a scourge to inflict injury on their own families. Neither were they able to understand that education gives the best chances to ability, but that education cannot be obtained without leisure. There were, however, many on the contrary who fully appreciated the benefits which the Factory Acts are calculated to bestow. They could see the advantages which a sober and well-regulated work people confer on society. They could see how baneful it was, both in itself and by example, for skilled hands, because they were skilled, to run riot every Monday and late into Tuesday, stopping all consecutive work to theirs, wasting the time and money of their fellow workers in the most unjustifiable manner and presenting what was far worse, a temptation and an example to others which was too often irresistible, and they were satisfied to wait the result, and to give me every assistance in their power.

Certain ceramic styles involved the use of toxic materials - none
more so than majolica introduced in the 1850s.

Few industries were as dependent on talent and skill as the ceramic industry of the 19th and
early 20th centuries. This finely painted tray, with a view of the Bay of Naples, is the work of
Daniel Lucas, Copeland, mid-19th century. *Both items by permission of The Potteries Museum.*

Reports of the Inspectors of Factories to Her Majesty's
Principal Secretary of State for the Home Department

Report of Robert Baker Esq., Inspector of Factories,
for the Nine Months ended the 31st of January, 1865.

The Potteries Proper, and Their Population.

By the census returns of 1861 there were employed in the manufacture of earthenware, in
the whole county of Stafford, which virtually means "The Potteries," 17,356 males, and
10,075 females 27,431. Less than four years ago, there were to be found working in the
potteries some of which I shall hereafter have to describe, and for the hours of work, of
which I shall have to speak, out of an aggregate number of both sexes of 27,432 not fewer
than 593 little children of five years old, of whom 159 were females, nor less than 4,605
other children of between five years old and ten, making altogether under ten years old an
aggregate number of 5,918 persons, of whom 2,917 were females.

In looking at the form and the helplessness of a child of five years old, one's own child
for example, it is scarcely to be believed that such a state of things could ever have existed,
and especially when the average wages of potters is taken into account. But these figures
are not of my collecting. I have, it is true, seen children of five years old at work, once in
the textile districts and now again in the potteries, and once again very recently in a
brickfield. And I have seen a good many children lately who were five when they first
commenced to work, though they are eight now. But the above are census enumerations,
and were taken from house to house, and it is my pleasure and privilege to add, that they
tell a tale, of which the happiest part is, that it can be told no longer. But they fully bear
out the statements made by the master potters in their memorial to Her Majesty's
government:

1. That children are employed in the potteries at a very early age, and in a way to interfere
injuriously with their education, and
2. That this state of things is the cause of various moral and physical evils to the youthful
population of the district.

The Different Branches of Pottery Employment

The divisional employment of potters is a matter of interest in many points of view, but
more particularly for the purpose of enquiring into those parts of it which are said to be not
only prejudicial to health and morals, but to life itself. With this idea, I endeavoured at the
outset to obtain a correct analysis of all the branches of labour in earthenware manufacture,
and the number of persons in each branch, in the form adopted under the Factory Act,
namely of adults, young persons between 13 and 18 years of age, and of children under 13
in each district separately. This analysis is so approximate to the census returns, being only
in excess of them by 456 persons that there can be no doubt of its accuracy. This excess
may be partially accounted for by the difference between the periods in which the returns

were taken, and partly by a number enumerated in my returns, which are not placed amongst "manufacturers of earthenware" in the census returns. We are thus enabled not only to apply remedial measures in the right direction but to separate the remainder of these departments from those which are deleterious, so as to relieve by far the largest portion from a correlative imputation which they do not deserve.

It has been seen that in 1861 the census number of persons engaged in the manufacture in the whole county of Stafford was 27,432. My returns make it at the present moment in the potteries proper 27,878.

Before, however, I proceed to speak of the potters generally, permit me to present to you an outline of one of the sub-divisions, Longton, which has the reputation of being the worst of all five, whether for its uncleanly condition, its want of ventilation or its workshops, or being the most backward in general intelligence, because, a description of it was and is, its houses, streets, properties and people, indicates somewhat the state out of which the other towns appear to be gradually rising, and also accounts for much of the architecture of the "banks" themselves. For my part, I do not agree with the censure which a comparison with the other pottery towns attempts to fasten upon Longton. It may be true that earthenware is to be had more cheaply there than elsewhere, and that its master potters are a little nearer the bench than the present generation of manufacturers in Stoke, Hanley, Burslem and Tunstall, but this I know, that there are "banks" as bad, and potters as vicious, to be found in any of these towns, as in Longton, and that many of them are bad enough, and vastly require rectification. Moreover, the present commercial status of Longton is but a few years old, and although a good deal remains to be done in the way of sanitary reforms and intellectual progress, much has been attempted that is eminently praiseworthy. In population it ranks only fourth of the five towns, but in number of "banks" it precedes them all. For the following information with respect to it, I am indebted to Mr. Palmer, a most intelligent resident in Longton, and my thanks are especially due to him for the great pains and care which he has bestowed upon his communication.

"In 1817", says he, "the township of Longton and Lane End contained population of 2,277 males and 2,653 females, making a total of 4930 inhabitants. The number of families was then 1,079, of houses 1,032, at the present time there are in Longton proper 3,860 properties, 3,606 of which are houses, 62 manufactories, 32 mills and offices, and 140 of a miscellaneous character, owned by 630 proprietors. At a much later period than this, the streets in the town were all unpaved, except two short lengths, which had been paved by the owners of the property. The channels were all open ditches, and many of the roads were in such a condition as to be scarcely passable, the ruts being so deep as to sink a conveyance up to its axle. Indeed, at this point, there were comparatively few portions of the town that arrogated themselves the title of streets. They were satisfied with the term 'lanes' characteristic of the locality they described, such as Hog's Lane, Smock Lane, Stir Pudding Row and Devil's Nook. Street lamps were not even dreamt of. Many of the houses were extremely rude in their construction, and unevenly built. They were all sorts, sizes and shapes. Scarcely a dozen houses throughout the town were uniform in height, style, and frontage. Background and foreground were made to blend in most grotesque confusion. Corners and gables, backs and fronts, all ranged in one street, and in but a few cases, those not unnecessary appendages to every well ordered house, the closet, the pigsty, the coal hole, and the stable, formed the foreground, even to modern Longton, with a dunghill and ashpit to relieve the picture.

Many of the houses were of very lowly pretensions. A man of six feet in stature could not stand in these domiciles in an erect position. These cottages were chiefly built of mud and stone, had thatched roofs, and windows and doors of very primitive type. The bed room and living room were both in one, or sometimes divided by a partition wall on the ground floor. The family washing was generally carried on on a kind of stone 'setlass' in front of the house. Nevertheless, these huts were frequently clean and snug, whitewashed within and without, and in them the comforts of life were often realised in a large degree.

At this time the character of the people, to a great extent, was in harmony with the place. The tastes of the masses were low and brutalising. The advantages of education were not realised. The prevailing amusements were bull-baiting, bear-baiting, dog-fighting, cock fights, men-fighting and race running, and consequent on these, drunkenness and its attendant vices existed to a large extent.

On political questions the people were excitable and violent. The creed of the lower classes was rabid chartism, and during elections a most malignant spirit manifested itself. I am proud, however, to say, that chartism is only known as a thing that was. Improved circumstances and better information have wiped out that stain from the character of the town for ever.

Yet, with all these odious features, there existed the genuine elements of a noble-hearted people, which distinguished themselves in protection to the weak, in a generous hospitality, and the bold espousal of an injured cause, and these only needed judicious guidance to make them things of worth. The good wanted cherishing and training, and the bad weeded out, and in the order of providence men have sprung up whose object in life has been to gently remodel the social and moral aspect of the population, and in this great and good work they have been marvellously successful. It is now patent to every observer that a great change for the better has come over the place and the people. The physical aspect of the town has been metamorphosed, and with every public improvement, a beneficial influence has been manifestly exerted upon the people. Their tastes have been elevated, their ambitions excited, and a desire for progress has been infused into their minds. The current of their pleasure has been turned into a proper channel. An onward march has been started in good earnest, and the changes already effected are but the faint foreshadowings of achievements yet to be accomplished.

Up to the year 1839 the town had no governing body. In that year a special act of parliament was obtained for lighting, watching and improving the town by commissioners. In 1855 these commissioners adopted the Nuisance Removal Act, and ever since have been most assiduous in the discharge of their duties. Up to June 1864, they have caused the owners of property to enlarge, repair, or erect 695 privies, cesspools, and ashpits, to open, cleanse, relay, or form 207 drains, soughs, or gutters, to remove 111 pigstyes which were too near dwelling houses, and to carry away 110 manure or other heaps of filth of an offensive or injurious character. They have caused the tenants of various properties in 772 instances to thoroughly cleanse and limewash their premises, and to remove, in 112 cases, pigeons, donkeys, fowls, dogs and rabbits from the interior of their dwelling houses. But to thoroughly eradicate existing or sanitary evils a complete system of drainage is essentially requisite. At the present time a very small portion of the town is drained, to meet this want there requires from seven to eight miles of sewerage, which might be completed for about £14,000."

These extracts from Mr. Palmer's report have been selected, as I have before said, with the view of exhibiting to you one of the towns and, by parity of reasoning, many of the places of work in it, with which I have had to deal in my official capacity. The 'banks' have indeed been formed, in many instances, of old premises, "rude in construction, unevenly built, and of all sorts, sizes, and shapes, background and foreground blending in grotesque confusion," and having been added to from time to time, as the necessity arose for greater accommodation, they now more resemble huge rabbit burrows than manufactories, for they are in and out, up and down, underground and attic, up rickety stairs and down in storage cellars, requiring a firm step and an aptitude to stoop, and sharp eye to enable one to see "round all corners", for the creatures, young and old, male and female, which are running here and there in every direction. And when I inform you that these banks extend by piecemeal, from a single room to over 15 acres, some idea may be formed of the difficulty of thoroughly inspecting them, and of the many points which have to be considered, and in every relative point of view, so as to enable me to carry out not only the clauses of the Act which restrict the labour of children and females, but those especial clauses which relate to sanitary requirements on which legislation has been attempted for the first time.

Of course 'banks' or parts of 'banks' that have been erected, and some of those which have always been occupied by wealthy proprietors, are not included in the description which I have just given. Those that I have referred to are mainly the workshops of men of small capital, who were once, and not long ago, workmen themselves, and who are unable, for want of means, to carry out the improvements in their premises, of which they do not fail to see the advantage and the necessity, as well as anybody else. Moreover, many of these premises are held under leases for terms of years, and the landlords are either too poor to improve them, or are unwilling to keep pace with the times, affirming that 'the old times were the best, and that what did for them might do well enough for those that came after them.'

There are, however, also a few better-to-do masters who are either indifferent to the comforts of their work people, or too idle to take even the decencies of life into consideration. I believe I speak without exaggeration when I say, that 40 per cent of all the banks which I have seen, and they have not been a few, were entirely without any accommodation for the female workers, and none that the men could use. Many of the yards too are formed of ashes, and in consequence of the transit over them of heavy-laden carts, there are deep ruts formed in them, which hold water after rain, into which the workers are liable to step in dark mornings and so to remain with wet feet for the whole day. I have also had to complain of defective drainage, of broken windows in the work rooms, by scores, rendering the workers liable to chest affections (sic) of every kind, and of dangerous steps for want of handrails, and of many other things which one would have thought the commonest care for their work people would have remedied instanter. I will not, however, weary you with more remarks upon these points, I will only make a few remarks from my diary, with reference to two or three of the "banks" which have fallen under my notice. The following letter received today: "Sir, I think it a Duity (sic) of mine to draw your attention to a great inconvenience, existing in the potters' manufactories generally. I can assure you there is but a very few Factories that as (sic) water closets fit for a female to go: and as I Here so Litle (sic) mention made, you will excuse me Drawing your attention to the Evil existing - Yours a working man, (quere woman?)".

"Visited Messrs..... Is a most fearful place. One of the partners attended and observed that if they left it, all the old places would fall in, and only the new remain. Here the privies for the men were in a most disgusting state, and there were none for the women. The rooms were also very small, low, and badly ventilated. Heat 120 deg. All the roadways were greasy, filthy, and altogether wretched. The excuse here, for this condition of the bank was, as elsewhere, that 'the landlord would do nothing' and that but for the act nothing ever would have been done, and the work people would have gone on in the same way as long as the places would have held together. Employ upwards of 250 work people, of whom 90 are females."

"Visited very old works. Girls of 16 wedging clay and lifting half a hundredweight at once, every few minutes, complained of being very tired. Wedged all day, and sometimes till 8 o'clock at night. There are many stoves in all. Rooms are very hot. No double doors to stoves. There are a few children under 11 working full time. Courts are not very clean, and some of the rooms appear as if they were about to fall, and have to be sutained (sic) with props in various ways. Of 18 girls and boys asked, 12 said 'they could not read, or could only read a bit.' The sagger-making place was so hot that it burst the bulb of a thermometer marked to 120 deg. Employ upwards of 100 people."

"Visited the works of..... Employ upwards of 120 people. Whilst there is a workman on the premises, not in working clothes and evidently disposed to be angry, pointed out to me the damp condition of the floor on which the workers stood all day - he amongst the rest - owing to a want of drainage in the yard, which was considerably above the floor of the workshop. The flags of the floor were very damp, and some of the workers had provided themselves with timber on which to stand. I also saw at this bank such an utter want of decency and disregard of the comforts of the work people as would not be believed were it not to be seen. The entrance to one of the principal workroom was under a sort of platform, to which there was an ascent by some outside steps of stone, lying parallel with the building, the pillar of those steps forming part of the entrance way. In the recess formed by these steps was a privy, with the door opening into the passage, not four feet wide, by which the people entered into this workroom, that not only could not decency be observed but privacy was out of the question, and the stench in the room was abominable."

'Visited the bank of.... The most wretched hole imaginable. There had been heavy rains during the night and walking in the yard of these works covered the heel with mud three inches high. Many of the workrooms were a step or two below the yard and having no drainage at the doors, the wet entered into them and made them exceedingly uncomfortable.

Most of the outside steps were without handrails and were thus exceedingly dangerous when used at night. The workrooms were very hot and comfortless and had not been whitewashed for years. In asking to see the privees here, I found only one horrible place for all the workers, without any doors in front of a place of work constantly in use, with the people passing up and down in sight of it in every direction, no accommodation whatever for females. The total number of persons employed being 150."

"Visited..... Comfortable in many respects. Airy and well whitewashed, but ventilators placed unintentionally directly in front of the faces of the work people, by which they suffered severely at times from face ache and toothache. Requested them to be altered which was immediately promised."

"Visited.... In these works there is very little left to be desired. They show what can readily be accomplished by a master who requires discipline and enforces it and who in return for obedience and good will exerts himself for the comfort of his work people. The courtyards are all paved, and every room and all the staircases are whitewashed once a year. Great pains have been taken to render the ventilation perfect. The floors also are as clean as they are capable of being kept in such works. Even the outer walls of the buildings within the curtilage are all cleaned once in every year. Nor can it be said that this is a result which is due to new works, for in all the old portions, of which there are several with very low rooms, the same order and cleanliness prevail. In many of the rooms many females, in some, all girls, in others, all women, are at work on the various processes of manufacture, but there is no loud talking and no disorder, and everywhere there seems, as there is, a discipline which evidences what may be accomplished where there is a will. The ventilation of the rooms is very fair. It is effected by openings to the external air of the size of a brick in the upper part of the walls, near the ceilings, which render the rooms of an agreeable temperature, and the workers look healthy. Most of the persons whom I saw at work were above 13 years old. The total number of persons employed is very large."

"Visited..... said to be the worst of all the banks in the potteries, and the facts do not very much belie the statements made against it. Over the whole of the works there was much dirt, endless broken windows, steam from the slip-maker's shop into the shops above through the floor, which yawned with great crevices everywhere, and the conductor, which ought to have carried the steam away, broke to pieces. Many children were employed here in hovels of every description, and in rooms in which there were stoves at almost every degree of heat, of which rooms the masters did not even profess to know the number, nor the number of his work people. There was no paving to the courts, which in wet weather must have been in a wretched condition, and several of his work people were working in rooms built around skeleton hovels, in which the heat in summer time must be intolerable. The stairs and steps of this wretched place were in many instances broken and in holes, and all without bannisters, so that at night and in winter the ascent and descent to the workrooms must be attended with considerable danger. No whitewashing had been ever put on these inside walls or ceiling, nor had the floors been swept apparently for months."

"Visited .....'s place, and was shown over his large works. Saw several children, principally under eleven, employed as mould runners. The works were light and airy, and cleaner than many. They had been regularly whitewashed, and were pretty well-ventilated. The stoves were numerous, and some of them as high as 110 deg."

"Visited .... Found it an old-fashioned place, of large area, which had once been in active operation, but of late years this had been somewhat diminished. The owner and occupier politely asked me to walk round with him, and invited my opinion on the various alterations which would be required in order to bring these works into full compliance with the law. I pointed out a want of spouts, drains, windows, broken floors, and a vast many other things of like nature, which had either gone to ruin, become stopped up, or had been originally disregarded, which I was afterwards informed had been estimated to cost £600, and was made a source of complaint against the Factory Act, the proprietor forgetting that this amount only pointed out the extent of his antecedent neglect.

The Potter's Employment. Its effect upon Health and suggested Remedies

I think there can be no doubt about the potters being physically 'a stunted race'. Whether this arises from the habits of the people, from their occupations, or from both, the fact, as asserted in the master's memorial to government, appears to me to be undeniable. The children, though working all day long in such variable temperatures, and hitherto for such occasional long hours, seem not without energy enough, as you see them playing in the streets at meal times, but their faces are pale and sallow, and their figures display none of those rounded curves by which happy and cared for childhood is so distinguished. They more resemble, than any other that I have seen, the children of widows in destitute circumstances or Irish children, that are fed on thin coffee, bread, and herrings. We could, indeed, scarcely expect to find, physiologically, that the children of such sensual parents should be otherwise than stunted, under the circumstances, first of their peculiar geniture, and, secondly, of wear and tear which is inconsistent with development. I do not, however, intend to refer to any of the various branches of this trade, as shown in the preceding tables, than those which are known to be more especially prejudicial to health, since it may be assumed, a priori, that all trades in which long hours of work obtain, are prejudicial to the physical moral health of those engaged in them.

And first of all, as to the hours of work. For years these appear to have been most irregular, depending upon the execution of shipping orders, or upon the drunkenness and dissipation of the heads of departments. Working by piecework, and bound to deliver over within so many days a certain sale of product, the laches of the early part of the week have had to be thrown over the latter part of it, and all the goods which could not be completed by the day, to be eked out at its close. The peculiarity of a potter's trade, namely, its being composed of consecutive branches, one branch being so thoroughly dependent on another, is unfortunate in this respect, it so easily leads to a derangement of the comforts of the many by the irregularities of the few. A workman, for example, who heads a department himself on a Monday or any other day of the week, stops by that absence all the branches which follow him. Thus, supposing there be no clay in stock, and the slip makers to absent

The second half of the 19th century witnessed an unprecedented demand for tiles of all kinds, a demand satisfied by the introduction of mechanisation from the 1830s. In this photograph women wearing protective clothing are shown applying lead-based majolica glazes.

The factory system turned pottery workers into specialists. Some benefited from this new status, while others were adversely affected by either constant exposure to dangerous substances or an unhealthy working environment.

themselves, all the workers on the "bank" would be stopped also, and have to sacrifice their wages on their account. On one occasion I was present when a workman had been newly hired for a year, and deemed that a fitting occasion for a "wetting", so he left his work at noon, having tempted a second fellow worker with him, and when I was on the "bank" seven others had been awaiting their return for hours, the total loss of wages to these people for that day being about 20s. Under the old regime, these workmen and these workers would have had to make up, by working late on Thursday and Friday nights, the loss of product occasioned by the escapade of Monday and Tuesday. In other cases, the execution of certain orders within a given time may have induced long hours, especially in certain departments. Some few weeks after the Factory Extension Act was passed, I entered a paintresses room at 7 o'clock p.m., and found 16 young girls all at work, which they were prepared to continue to 9 o'clock, "according to orders, as the ware was wanted," and it was only on my asserting that the masters would be punished if they did, that the work was abandoned. Thus, on another occasion, I detected on the language of the workman that he had a night set as well as a day set, and that notwithstanding the law, night work was still practised. I felt that this was a case for prosecution, and accordingly the firm was brought before the stipendiary magistrate, but I instructed the sub-inspector to withdraw the case, as it was the first, on condition that the practice should not be continued.

Generally speaking, in the textile districts there are but few applicants for leave to change the hours of work in the winter months from 6 till 6 to 7 till 7, but in the potteries this change has been almost universal during this winter. Whether it will be continued or not through another winter is doubtful, for the change disturbs the domestic habits of a family in the morning, and deprives the night schools of occupants in the evening, without adequate compensation. For the first winter it was well enough, but when the workers once become accustomed in the spring and summer mornings to the early rising, which 6 to 6 o'clock enforces, and to the refreshing exercise which may be obtained when work is over, it is probable that they will retain these hours, which the habit will, by that time, have induced them to continue.

The following are the processes which have been said to be unhealthy:

Slip making
1. By the wet rooms and wet standing places which it occasions, and
2. By the steam which is generated during the process. The slip maker is a person who prepares the materials for use, and this he does by one of two processes, either by plunging the clay in water with a wooden instrument, till the whole is of the consistence of thick cream, and afterwards boiling it upon a kiln till it is very similar in appearance to glazier's putty, or, by machinery, of which there are as yet few instances, which, first of all, grinds the flints to powder, then mixes them with water in large troughs to the cream consistence, then strains them through fine gauze, and delivers them eventually to hydraulic presses, by which the same putty consistence is obtained. No doubt the latter process is far more healthy and effective, and time and capital are only required to bring it into general use. It will probably initiate machinery, in the manufacture of earthenware, for when once steam power has been adopted on a pot "bank", hydraulic slip making, and machinery generally,

will follow as a matter of course. There are 618 slip makers in the potteries, and the average age which they attain, assuming that their occupation is not instrumental to dissipated habits, appears not to exceed 52 years, and it may be justly therefore considered and unhealthy branch. Out of 11 slipmakers who died in 1864, three lived to above 60 years of age, and six died of asthma and bronchitis.

Flat Pressers
1. Including Jigger Turners and Mould Runners. By the heat which the stoves occasion, and from which they are not duly protected in the workrooms
2. In the operation of jigging.
3. In the operation of mould running.
4. In the operation of wedging clay.
The total number of flat pressers and their attendants appears to be 3,828 males and 500 females, of whom 1,078 males and 191 females are young persons, and 1,765 males and 285 females, children. If we add the young persons and children together we include all the jigger turners and mould runners, and they amount to 3,319, of whom 476 are females. These figures are interesting, for it must be remembered that in 1861 the census returns, which included all that were really working, though perhaps some only occasionally, gave the number of these children at 593 of five years old, and not less than 4,605 as between five and ten years old. It thus appears to be self-evident that, in the selection of the Mining Act as that which was to restrict labour, the maximum physical capability of a child was the object estimated, and that the educational power, or opportunities of the children themselves, were either omitted from the estimate, on the supposition that by the time it was ten years old a child might be sufficiently educated for all its future requirements, or that the education in return for an indispensable form of labour, was a thing to be disavowed. These figures show, I think, conclusively also, the fallacy of the outcry with respect to the impossibility of obtaining two sets of children for the half-time system. It was asserted broadly by the advocates for the Mining Act, and is now by others who are adverse to the educational clauses of the Factory Act, that ten years old was and is the only admissable age for a child to work on an earthenware bank. But if so, then it would seem, by the parents' showing, that of the children employed in such establishments at the time of the census, fully nine tenths of those who were at that time between five and ten years old, and all those under five years old, would have had to be discharged, and to be replaced by others who were fully ten, exactly doubling the numbers with the reduction of the age to eight years on the half-time principle, and very greatly increasing the cost of production to the workman.

As to the flat pressers alone, it is very difficult from the returns to divide them into adults and adolescents, but at a reasonable estimate they amount to 1,500, and their employment is doubtless prejudicial in two ways, one of which is due to the kind of labour, the other to moral causes.
1st. By the heat in which they work, and
2nd. By the inducement to drunkenness which that heat and habit together, occasion, the former of the two assisting most materially to develop, and promote the latter. Of 65 flat pressers who died in 1864, in Longton, Fenton, Hanley, Stoke, and Shelton, 27 died of

phthisis, 10 of bronchitis, 4 of asthma, 4 of pneumonia, 3 of apoplexy, 3 of dropsy, and the rest of different ailments, so that of the total 70 per cent died of diseases of the chest, and the average age of each person did not exceed 41 years.

A more startling confirmation of the evidence given to Mr. Commissioner Longe by Mr. Bilton, the manager of the Copeland Works, could hardly have been contemplated. Mr. Bilton's words are these: "the greatest good the legislature could do, if it were possible, would be to bring about a change in the present system of stoves." And again, "I think the heat of the stoves is the great evil of the trade. I believe it is the cause of drinking habits as well as of the debilitated constitutions which prevail among potters."

It is not to be anticipated that there would be found a corresponding ratio of deaths among the children as among the adults, even though working within the mischief of the same causes. The seeds are only sown in childhood which require years to mature. But they are sown then, and are as certainly brought to maturity, or we should find the average age of the pottery population much higher than it is.

With respect to the ages at which I have seen children at work, they vary. I have seen two or three at five years old, several at six and seven years, and a great many at between eight and eleven years of age. I have been told by many that they commenced work when they were only five years old, thus confirming the census returns. Their answers were given first, as to their ages, then as to the length of time they had been employed altogether. On questioning one little fellow who began to work at that early age, as to the distance he came, I was replied to by another of the same small stature as himself, that when he came to work as a 'jigger" he walked a mile and a half each way to work for his brother, when he himself was in petticoats. Another child who was not yet six years old when I saw him at another bank, informed me that he could not read, that he had been "jigging" for sometime, and that he worked the previous night till 8 o'clock pm. In another instance I was rather struck with the confident tone in which a manufacturer assured me that in his establishment no child under eight years old had ever been employed. When on passing a very small child at work, I said, "How old are you?" "Going nine, sir, he replied. "Yes", answered the manufacturer, "that is so". "But", said I, "how long have you worked here?" "Three years," was the answer, which proved to be the fact.

In conversing with the manufacturers on the numbers of very small children seen upon their premises, the almost invariable answer was (as it used to be among the woollen people in 1833) that "they did not employ them," that the men find their own attendants and pay them, and that they, the masters, have no control over them: and thus they attempt to get rid of the responsibility of this infantile employment. But the fact is, that, as they can and do discharge these children on the instant, and have discharged numbers who would have had to be sent to school had they been retained, so they might have discharged all the children at five years old that used to work before the act was passed, had the moral question of their employment been impressible upon them.

The days will come, I presume, and sooner now than they would have done had the Factory Act not been introduced among the potters, when "jigging" or turning the potter's wheel, will be performed by machinery. In two instances only have I seen it hitherto. In one, where it has been in operation for some years, in another, where it has but just been introduced, but was standing for a very singular reason. As I understood, the introduction of this machinery had done away with the labour of one boy at each machine, and as the workman works by piece and pays his own attendants, so the cost of production had been lessened to the workman at the machinery by one boy each, or at the rate of about 2s.6d. a workman per week, and this sum was therefore imposed as a rent upon the machine, which the workman was expected to pay, the other advantages of the machine being deemed compensatory for this reduction. This demand on the part of the master had been refused by the workman and so all the machinery was standing. There are objections, however, to the immediate use of machinery for pottery purposes, which may postpone its introduction for some time yet. It requires, as it appears to me, a more educated class of workmen, a finer touch to regulate the speed, and a juster idea of the economy of power than as yet overspreads the minds of the potters generally. Moreover, it requires an outlay of which it will be difficult to impress the necessity on the minds of the masters, and last, and not least, it will require new buildings altogether in a majority of the "banks" to render its employment available and free from danger.

The children who work for the flat pressers are employed, first, in turning the wheel on which the workman forms the ware on moulds made of plaster of Paris, second, in carrying the moulds with the ware upon them into an adjoining closet built within the flat presser's room, where there is a stove heated to a very high temperature, often as high as 141 deg. fahrenheit, and there placing them on shelves to dry, and thirdly, in wedging the clay which the potters use. I could not use more exact terms in describing this employment, nor the reasons why the heat should be so excessive, than those which Mr. Longe has used, namely: "These stoves are little rooms, or rather ovens, of about 13 feet square, and from 8 to 12 feet high, partitioned off from the shop. They are fitted inside with shelves, on which the moulds, with the moist ware upon them, are placed, in order that the ware may be dried sufficiently to be removed. In the centre is the stove, which I have often observed red hot. As the potter forms the plate or saucer on the mould, the mould runner runs off with it to the "stove". In proportion as the number of moulds with which the workman is supplied is limited, has the heat of the stove to be raised, in order that the moulds may be more quickly dried, so as to be used again. Besides entering to place the moulds, the boy has also to enter to turn them, in order that the ware may not be hurt in drying.

As in overcoming most of the difficulties which arise in trade operations when first placed under legal restrictions, the questions are those of appliances more than anything else, so it is also in the construction and management of these stoves. There would never need to be excessive heat in any of the flat presser's stoves, if there were moulds enough for the workman's supply. But as these moulds are somewhat expensive and cumbersome for storage, and are often not very carefully used by the workmen, so, where fuel is plentiful, their supply is limited to the smallest number consistent with the ware to be produced, and the stove is heated in proportion to the deficiency of moulds to be used. But when fuel is scarce and these moulds can dry, as it were, at leisure, their supply is more abundant, the question of the health of the mould runners not often being an element of consideration. Moreover, the construction of many of these stoves is as bad as it can well be, for the health of all the workers engaged about them. In a well-regulated room (and I speak now entirely of the general system of stoveage) and even with a somewhat limited supply of moulds, the heat, though considerable, is not excessive. The stove is built close up to the top of the ceiling, the ceiling above being underdrawn, in order to protect the feet of the worker overhead, and the little doors by which the mould runner makes his exit and entrance are double, and so hung as to fall both ways, thus retaining the heat within the stove itself, as far as is possible. But the exceptions to this rule, which are unfortunately very numerous, are, that the outside walls of the stoves are only partially carried upwards, so that there is, perhaps, a 2ft. opening over the top of them, that there are no doors to them, or, if there are, they are off their hinges, or that they only open one way, and are consequently always open, and thus the heat, which should be limited to the area of the stove for all purposes both useful and economical, is thrown into the whole room, till it is almost suffocating. The physical condition of these children, who are thus passing momentarily in and out of these stoves, may be imagined, the moral and mental can be scarcely less patent to any considerate mind. As I have said before, we only do not thus see the results of disease, from the resistance which young and vigorous life is capable of making against its inroads, but we may trace the elements of it in the evidences of wear and tear which, as I have shown before, these children prematurely exhibit. I quite agree with many of the witnesses who gave evidence before the commissioners, that girls should never be employed as mould runners or jigger turners, and I trust to be able hereafter to report that the practice has been discontinued.

This old system of stoveage is, however, on the wane, and must shortly disappear altogether. There are already four or five other systems at work ready to supersede it, in all of which the heat is generated with a due regard to economy, and without its being at all needful that even the mould runner should come in injurious contact with it. In Messrs. Minton's establishment, most of the evils which accrue from the old system of stoveage are done away. They have erected a stove in one room, and others are to follow, consisting of a circular chamber built in one of the rooms, and supplied with heat by a brick flue the fireplace being nothing more than an ordinary grate, and the flue, similar to that used for a greenhouse. The fire is fed from the flat presser's workroom, just as that of a copper is in a kitchen, and the flue passes round the bottom of this circular chamber. Then within the area formed by the flue is a large wheel, like the paddle wheel of a steam boat inverted, revolving on a perpendicular shaft. This wheel is encircled with shelves, which are capable of containing as many dishes or plates, or pieces of ware, as are made by the workmen of these rooms in a day. On these shelves, the moulds are placed through sliding doors, which, when lifted up, expose the shelves as the wheel revolves. When the wheel is quite full, all these sliding doors are kept shut, the moulds are left for a while to dry (whilst another wheel is being filled) and are afterwards removed and renewed.

The Jigger Turner
The labours of the jigger turner are not limited to mould running and jigger turnings but include also wedging and carrying clay, in which latter operation, I regret to say, I have seen several young females employed, so frequently indeed, that I have been obliged to do that which is tantamount to forbidding it. The law enables me to seek the opinion of the

certifying surgeon in any case in which I observe a child employed on any work which appears to me beyond its strength, and if he thinks it is, its certificate may be cancelled so that the child can no longer be employed illegally, and the master become subjected to a penalty. On the 2nd. November last, my attention was more particularly called to this kind of employment, by the following letter from one of the certifying surgeons:

"I saw at a manufactory yesterday, a thin delicate looking girl of twelve, who was to run moulds, turn the jigger, and carry on her head ten or twelve times during the morning, from 50 to 60lbs. weight of clay, for a considerable distance. In my opinion no girl ought to be required to perform such an act. The employers say, in many instances, the weights placed upon the girls are more than they can carry and that they are not infrequently (sic) obliged to drop them by the way. One manufacturer asked me the other day if the act contained any provision for preventing girls from working at this particular employment altogether, as he was persuaded it was one of the greatest evils existing in the trade, that the girls were frequently required to exert themselves far beyond their physical capabilities, and that the moral atmosphere to which they were exposed was something awful.'

The operation of clay wedging, or beating out the remaining air after the clay has been boiled or pressed, is wholly unfit for little children, and especially for female children, unless it is done by very small divisions of the material at a time. A little boy or girl may be required to lift 40 or 60lbs. of clay as high as it can reach, and then dash it down upon a table with all the force it can exercise and this continuously the day through. The wedge of clay is then cut in two with a piece of wire and re-wedged, and so on until it is finished. Many of the girls whom I saw thus wedging, complained of the excessive fatigue which it occasioned. A workman, speaking of it, observed "That was the work which soon made young people old."

"Clay wedging" says another of the certifying surgeons, "is in my opinion too laborious an occupation for boys and girls under 14 years of age, when followed during the greater part of the day with little or no intermission. In the case of girls, it is assuredly, to say the least, an inappropriate occupation, viewed apart from the question of their ability to pursue it.

"It should be interdicted to females under 16 years of age and to male children as defined by the Factory Act.

"It is a rude unskilful process in which no conditions are perceptible which may not be as completely fulfiled by the agency of some simple piece of mechanism.

"There can be no doubt, I think, that the process of wedging clay involves a repeated forcible interruption of the function of respiration, and that this interruption must be in some measure prejudicial to the lungs, and must react somewhat injuriously upon the heart, where this sort of labour is persisted in daily, and it is not impossible that from this cause arises asthma and the diseases of the heart and large blood vessels which are to be found in the death registers of the potteries.

"The injurious effects of wedging will be produced in a higher degree in children and in young persons under 14 years of age, inasmuch as the bony framework of the chest has in such, not yet acquired its firmness and solidity, and as the cell structure of the lungs is still extremely delicate and predisposed to injurious influences."

"The act of wedging involves the unnatural distension of the air cells and a longer retention of air in them than natural, followed by forcible expulsion, conditions which are favourable to the production of an asthmatic condition."

Dippers
The dipping occupation is one which is exceedingly injurious to health, the effects varying with different constitutions. The departments in which the workers are most subject to the poison of lead, which is used in dipping as a glaze, are the dippers and their assistants, the ware gatherers, ware brushers, glost placers, and ground-layers. Lead is largely used in the potteries for purpose of glazing the ware, and in various ways becomes absorbed into the systems of the workers. And though it is stated that the quantity consumed nowadays is by no means so large as formerly, still there is sufficient to produce material results as regards disease, and therefore to require such measures as may tend to diminish the effects of that absorption, and to counteract them as much as possible. In the manufacture of earthenware, lead is generally imbibed either by inhalation, by habitual contact with its compounds on the skin, or by the accidental introduction of them into the stomach with the food. In whatever way it is introduced, the effects of it are,
1. Functional disease of the alimentary canal:
2. Paralysis of some of the muscles:
3. Ulceration of the gums and sockets of the teeth, accompanied by a peculiar blue line, seen to run along the margin of the gums, but is absent where a tooth or stump is wanting.

This blue line is what Dr Christison calls "a warning symptom", and it so much so that if it were attended to as it deserves to be by the workers themselves, timely measures might be taken by them to prevent further mischief, a mischief which is exceedingly apt to recur when once it has acquired a complete form, and the system is re-exposed to the same influences, and to lead to a species of apoplexy which ends fatally, or to a partial paralysis, which renders further labour impossible. This species of paralysis affects chiefly the upper extremities, and is attended with excessive muscular emaciation. The loss of power and substance is most remarkable in the muscles which supply the thumb and fingers. On inquiry, I have found some of the dippers complain of several of these symptoms. The blue line indicating the absorption of lead is very common, colica pictonum not so much so, though a few have had it, and partial paralysis of the fingers or wrists is not unusual. Among the patients of the North Staffordshire Infirmary the blue line indication is so common as almost to cease to be remarkable.

It is no doubt true, that the susceptibility to lead poisoning varies very much with the different idiosyncrasies subjected to it. Some will bear to work amongst lead preparations for years without any serious results accruing from it, others again will suffer from a single day's contact with it. But sooner or later colic comes on, the wrists drop, or the ball of the thumb is painful, unless prophylactic measures are resorted to at the onset, and continued at intervals, in order to prevent any accumulation of the mineral in the system, and to release it of it. Dr Watson writes of this blue line as a capital sign by which workers in lead may be cautioned as to the absorption of this poison, and of the necessity of some treatment by which its effects may be avoided

The total number of persons in the potteries who are more or less exposed to the influence of lead, amounts to 1,136 males and 267 females. Of this number, only about 700 are employed in immediate contact with it in a fluid state, supposing that mineral to form an invariable ingredient in the glaze used.

With respect to the danger of its absorption by food, the law has provided specially "that at no time after the passing of this act shall any child, young person or woman be allowed to take his or her meals in the dipping houses, dipper's drying rooms, or china scouring rooms." But it falls short of the really prophylactic measures necessary to prevent the effects of lead poison among those who form the largest number of workers among the mineral, I mean the adult men. No part of the factory laws directly interferes with the labour of men it is true, but this precautionary measure might have gone beyond this limit, and have included them also in these mealtime regulations.

Thus the dipper, whose hands are most days, for hours, covered with lead compounds held in suspension, washes them probably, when he ceases to work and when he goes to his meals, but he dries them on his apron which is already thoroughly impregnated with lead from splashes occasioned by his manipulations. He will tell you that he uses a nail brush to his skin and nails as soon as he arrives at home. But I should prefer that he should use one also at the works before he goes home, for the process of absorption is sometimes a very rapid one. I have therefore requested that slop sinks, soap, clean water, nail brushes and towels shall be provided by the employers on the works, and that the dippers and their assistants shall be instructed how to use them properly.

Scouring

The operation of scouring has long been a source of considerable anxiety, not only to the manufacturer but to the operatives, for it is one of an almost certainly fatal character if persisted in. One master potter assured me that he had lost 15 girl scourers in 16 years.

The operation consists in divesting the ware of the fine flint powder in which it has been fired, but in so doing the fine dust flies in clouds about the heads and persons of the scourers until they are quite white with it, and as a considerable quantity is inevitably inhaled, bronchial irritation is set up which ends in diseases of the lungs and death.

General Want of Ventilation

I found in pottery rooms many ineffectual attempts at ventilation by the employers, evidencing not only the necessity but their desire for its accomplishment. But some of the workrooms are very small, formed as they have been out of the old cottage dwellings to which I have before adverted, or of other improvised rooms, in which the accommodation in it was originally sufficient has long been inadequate for the purposes to which they are now applied. In some banks workshops have been placed around skeleton hovels, two storeys high, and so closely are they built round that part of the chimney where the fire breaks out of the oven that they render the wall of the chimney excessively hot when the oven is at work, so hot indeed that it is next to impossible, without great danger to the health of the worker, to permit employment in such places. Yet many females are employed in them all day long, and especially in the summer months when the heat is greatly augmented, with a thermometer probably ranging from ninety degrees upwards. In the flat pressing rooms also, excessive heat prevails, as well as in many of the printing shops in which very small female children are sometimes crowded with other workers within the smallest possible space. In several of the other shops in which groups of people are assembled, there is considerable heat, but in these, it is not so much a diminished temperature as a better system of ventilation which is required. In the first of these cases, namely around the skeleton hovels, I have requested that no worker may be placed where there is not eight clear feet between the back of the worker and the brickwork of the hovel. No manufacturer who is at all considerate about his work people would allow them to work in such a situation under any circumstances, and by most of them it is very strongly condemned.

p.794 Note re dogs on factory premises:

With respect to the introduction of dogs into the workshops, perhaps less may be said with respect to the legal power of prohibition. As a matter of discipline it seems one of these nuisances which ordinary firmness would remove.

Following the wedging stage, clay was distributed to various departments on a factory by young boys and women. This photograph from *Cup and Saucer Land*.

The working areas within many factories were often cramped,
overcrowded and lacking adequate ventilation.

Samuel Scriven, a government inspector sent to investigate child labour in the Potteries during
the 1840s, encountered children as young as five years employed to perform a variety of
unskilled tasks. When this photograph was taken towards the end of the 19th century
government legislation was in force to limit the employers' use of child labour. Several
contributors to my interviews were working in the industry before the age of thirteen.

This photograph, taken at some point during the 1880s, provides interesting evidence concerning the lax conditions reported by the factory inspectorate. Both Scriven and Baker mention having seen babies and very young children crawling amongst dangerous machinery. Workers were also frequently disciplined for taking dogs onto factory premises.

The fettling of unfired and fired
wares was a source of silicosis
amongst many workers. The
problem was compounded by
careless working habits and
poor or non-existent ventilation.

A girl clay wedger from the
Rev. Graham's *Cup and Saucer
Land*. It was still common
place to find someone so
employed many years after the
date of this photograph, c.1900.

Both Scriven and Baker report seeing children as young as five employed to carry out a variety of unskilled tasks. This photograph, taken sometime during the 1890s, is from Rev. Graham's *Cup and Saucer Land.*

Wares were often placed in flint during the biscuit firing. Removal of the flint prior to being dipped in glaze involved a procedure known as scouring. It was a major cause of silicosis amongst those so employed.

Conclusion

Samuel Scriven's job in coming to North Staffordshire was to collect information from workers in the region's principal industry, in the most economical way. This meant, in its essentials, a short description of their duties and treatment at the hands of those who employed or supervised them. Someone charged with a similar responsibility today might prefer to use a questionnaire to collect information rather than the very time consuming one to one interview technique adopted by Scriven. Needless to say the use of a questionnaire in the 1840s would have presupposed an ability to read and write amongst the working population at large. That this was obviously not the case ruled out any approach other than direct contact between the inspectors and their target group.

What started out for me as an investigation into the subject of job satisfaction was expanded into an exercise with a wider agenda. My contributors' reminiscences were not limited to their work but included family details and references to the environment beyond the factory. Although the resulting interviews provided a rich collection of interesting memories it must be admitted that they would not, however, qualify as being a scientifically accurate sample. People were, after all, volunteering to talk about their life and work. The workers seen by Scriven were presumably systematically located and questioned.

Most of my interviewees recalled past events, and their work experiences with pleasure and a strong sense of nostalgia. However, someone with a negative perspective on their life might have lacked the motivation to come forward.

Certain contributors, notably Reginald Haggar and Reginald Tomlinson, had little to say about whether they enjoyed their work but given its artistic nature would lead one to assume that they did. My reasons for including the Haggar interview are because it provides, amongst other things, a most interesting historical overview from someone with direct experience of most of the situations described. In Reginald Tomlinson's case I find his testimony interesting for two main reasons (a) that he describes an activity which was quite rare in North Staffordshire in the early 1900s, namely that of being involved in the production of Art Pottery in a studio context, and (b) the need for caution in dealing with contentious information that one might be tempted to accept on trust because of the status of the contributor.

It should also be said that, with the exception of Mrs Foxall and Mr Hosey, most of the people I talked to considered their work to have been dependent on skill, and monetary considerations apart, largely rewarding. Had I, for example, received the testimony of a sliphouse labourer it would most probably have emphasised the more unpleasant aspects of the job, such as working with icy cold water in winter. Sliphouse work would also appear quite low on any scale based upon a hierarchy of skills.

Whether or not anyone enjoys their work will vary depending on attitude and circumstances. Some people adapt well to the performance of routine tasks, for example lathe treading, while others require variety. The quality that characterised the more positive amongst the men and women I interviewed was an admirable strength of character, developed in an age when independence and staying power were necessary for survival.

Appendix 2
Weekly Wages in the Ceramic Industry 1841-1938

Worker	s.
Thrower	40
Painter of landscapes and flowers	40
Platemaker	38
Turner	32
Dipper	32
Presser	30
Slipmaker	29
Warehouseman	24
Gilder	24
Groundlayer	24
Ovenman	18
Sliphouseman	18
Lathe-treader	10
Scourer	10
Transferrer	10
Children	$2^1/_2$d (average)

Weekly Wages in the Ceramic Industry 1877, 1908 & 1924

Worker	1877		1908		1924	
	s	d.	s	d.	s	d.
Thrower	37	6	27	10	76	2
Turner	29	0	26	10	58	9
Handler	28	0	28	2	52	4
Hollow-ware Presser	28	0	24	9	48	5
Flat-ware Presser	28	0	28	9	55	5
Mouldmaker	28	0	38	0	68	0
Printer	24	0	24	3	51	0
Jiggerer			35	1	67	9
Ovenman			30	0	56	4

The average earnings in 1924 in these trades were 59s. 4d., in the same year the average possible earnings (for a 47 hr week) were 73s. 8d.

Average Earnings in the Ceramic Industry 1938

Men	116s. 8d.
Youths and boys	40s. 5d.
Women	48s. 4d.
Girls	21s. 9d.

Some books available from Churnet Valley

BRINDLEY GENEALOGY Gordon Brindley	£12.95
BRITTAIN'S PAPER MILLS AND PAPERMAKING Robert Milner	£ 8.95
BULLERS OF MILTON Sue Taylor	£12.95
BURSLEM IN WORDS & PICTURES Mervyn Edwards	£ 8.95
DISTINCTIVE SURNAMES OF N. STAFFS I: From placenames and landscape E. Tooth	£ 9.95
DISTINCTIVE SURNAMES OF N. STAFFS II: From occupations, trades, rank & office	£ 9.95
DISTINCTIVE SURNAMES OF N. STAFFS III: From nicknames Edgar Tooth	£12.95
DURATION MAN A.J.Heraty A Staffordshire Soldier in the 1st World War	£ 7.95
EARTH MYSTERIES OF THE THREE SHIRES Doug Pickford	£ 7.95
ETRURIA: Jaspers, Joists and Jillivers Joan Morley	£12.95
FAMOUS WOMEN OF NORTH STAFFORDSHIRE Patricia Pilling.	£ 6.95
FARMERS AND POTTERS Gary Cooper	£ 7.95
GIVE MY REGARDS TO THE BROADWAY Barry Blaize	£ 8.95
GREAT PUBS AROUND STOKE ON TRENT Mervyn Edwards	£ 7.95
HOLLAND, JAMES Steve Bond Famous Victorian watercolourist from Burslem	£ 9.95
JAMES TRUBSHAW, Life and Works of :Builder and Architect Anne Bayliss	£ 4.95
KEELE, OFF THE RECORD A People's History of Keele Angela Drakakis-Smith	£ 8.95
LIEUTENANT HARRY LOFT, 64TH REG OF FOOT (2ND STAFFS) Martin Loft	£ 9.95
MILTON MEMORIES Florence Chetwin and Margaret Reynolds.	£ 8.95
MONASTIC STAFFORDSHIRE John L Tomkinson Religious houses of the County.	£12.95
MOTHER BURSLEM Bertram Hodgkiss An in depth history	£14.95
OVER THERE J.E. Blore & J.R. Sherratt. The Old Leek Battery 1908-1919.	£ 8.50
A POTTERIES LAD Bill Ridgway	£ 8.95
POTTERS AT PLAY Mervyn Edwards	£ 6.95
POTTERS IN PARKS Mervyn Edwards	£ 6.95
POTTERS IN PITS Mervyn Edwards	£ 6.95
POTTERS IN PUBS Mervyn Edwards	£ 6.95
PSYCHIATRY IN NORTH STAFFORDSHIRE Edward D Myers	£14.95
QUARRIES OF CAULDON LOW 2000 Basil Jeuda	£12.95
ROCESTER, A HISTORY OF Alan Gibson	£ 8.95
SHIP WITHOUT WATER Graham Bebbington HMS Daedalus II, Clayton, WW2	£ 8.95
SILVERDALE: LIFE ON THE DALE Barry Williams.	£ 8.95
ST EDWARD'S HOSPITAL, CHEDDLETON Max Chadwick & Dave Pearson	£20.00
STAFFORDSHIRE LEGENDS Alan Gibson	£ 8.95
MILLENNIUM EMBROIDERIES A History of Staffordshire Everitt & Mannering	£ 9 95
STAFFORDSHIRE REGIMENTS: Imperial, Regular & Volunteer 1705-1919 Dave Cooper	£12.95
STAFFORDSHIRE REGIMENTS II: 1705-1919 "The Scrapbook" Dave Cooper	£12.95
A CROWN FOR STAFFORDSHIRE Dianne Mannering	£12.95
STAFFORDSHIRE REGIMENT IN THE CRIMEA Robert Hope	£14.95
WHEN I WAS A CHILD Charles Shaw (1904) Illustrated edition	£12.95
WOLSTANTON IN WORDS AND PICTURES Mervyn Edwards	£ 8.95